Instructional Rounds in Education

Instructional Rounds
in Education

A NETWORK APPROACH TO IMPROVING
TEACHING AND LEARNING

ELIZABETH A. CITY

RICHARD F. ELMORE

SARAH E. FIARMAN

LEE TEITEL

HARVARD EDUCATION PRESS
CAMBRIDGE, MASSACHUSETTS

Sixth Printing, 2010.

Copyright © 2009 by the President and Fellows of Harvard College

Library of Congress Control Number 2008942554

Paperback ISBN 978-1-934742-16-7
Library Edition ISBN 978-1-934742-17-4

Published by Harvard Education Press,
an imprint of the Harvard Education Publishing Group

Harvard Education Press
8 Story Street
Cambridge, MA 02138

Cover Design: Perry Lubin

The typefaces used in this book are Adobe Minion Pro for text and Adobe Myriad Pro and ITC Fenice for display.

To the members of the Cambridge Leadership Network,
the Connecticut Superintendents' Network,
the Iowa Leadership Academy Superintendents' Network,
and the Ohio Leadership Collaborative,
who purposefully pursue their own learning
in order to be better leaders in their classrooms,
schools, and districts.

CONTENTS

FOREWORD

Reading a book in which your professional work is the object of study is an out-of-body experience. *Instructional Rounds in Education* tells the story of four networks—including the one with which I am affiliated—that use instructional rounds to improve teaching and learning.

My involvement with instructional rounds and Richard Elmore dates back to my tenure as executive assistant to superintendents Tony Alvarado and Elaine Fink in New York City's Community School District 2 during the 1990s. When I became executive director of the Connecticut Center for School Change, a statewide school support organization with a mission to improve teaching and learning, I recruited Elmore to co-develop with the center an executive leadership program for superintendents that would build on what he and I had learned about professional development and large-scale instructional improvement.

Initially, the Connecticut Superintendents' Network involved eight superintendents meeting in bimonthly, three-hour seminars to discuss the leverage points—resources, time, accountability, professional development—that superintendents have to improve their districts and to create the conditions that foster student achievement. After six months of prodding about the need to venture out from the comfort of a conference room and observe teaching and learning in classrooms, one member courageously volunteered to host a school visit. The visit demonstrated the power of rounds, and the network's current configuration took shape. Today, the network is a true community of practice, a group of twenty-six superintendents engaged in rounds. They share a common interest in learning how to foster and sustain improvements in the quality of instruction and in student learning.

The center created and nurtured the network because we have a vision of high-performing school systems in which all students are performing at high levels and in which all components of the organization—personnel, finances, curriculum, and assessment—are focused on instructional improvement. That vision is summed up in our motto: "System Success = Student Success." As described in this book, rounds—with its focus on the instructional core, a collaborative culture that values reflection and adult learning, and a coherent theory of action and a systemwide implementation strategy—can be an effective tool for achieving that vision of large-scale instructional improvement.

The center has sponsored the network for eight years. The objectives of the Connecticut Superintendents' Network are, first, to develop the knowledge and skill of superintendents to lead large-scale instructional improvement; and, second, to help superintendents focus their organizations and systems on their core purpose: student learning. The participating superintendents clearly feel the network is value-added, as evidenced by their 90 percent attendance record, their continued commitment to participate, and their financial support (membership fees run from $2,700 to $4,000 annually and cover half the cost of program expenses). While that is a testament to the quality of the professional development that the center provides, it is fair to ask, as we do all the time, the "so what?" question. What has been the impact of instructional rounds on superintendents' practice, their districts, and teaching and learning? Our theory of action is: If we collectively participate in a community of practice grounded in *on-site* classroom observation and focused on large-scale instructional improvement, *then* participating superintendents will become more effective instructional leaders as demonstrated by changes in their practice, and, ultimately, improvements in student achievement.

Our evaluators tell us that the network and rounds have led to changes in beliefs and practices. The superintendents recognize that teaching and learning is job number one and that it just can't be delegated to a deputy or to principals. The superintendents are spending more time in classrooms, aligning budget and human resources with their theories of action, and using some of the tools and protocols back in their districts to extend the learning to other administrators. Principals in their districts consistently stress the importance of data-driven instructional decisions. Analysis of transcripts of the network's sessions indicates that over time, the members have improved in their ability to observe classroom practice and stay in the descriptive voice, to build on the conversational thread of the discussion, and to analyze observational data and recommend the next level of work. The main issues the network consistently needs to address, regardless of the socioeconomic status of the district, are these: Are teachers or students doing the work? What is the level of rigor and challenge of the tasks students are asked to do? Can you hear student voice in classroom discourse? What role do leadership teams have in educational improvement?

As a network, we've learned several things:

- Teaching matters most.
- An effective theory of action connects the central office and the classroom.
- Systemic improvement is not linear.
- Districts need to continuously measure progress.
- Solutions must be adapted to local contexts.
- Modeling alone is not sufficient; accountability counts.
- Communities of practice accelerate learning.
- External assistance is helpful.

Reading *Instructional Rounds in Education: A Network Approach to Improving Teaching and Learning* will give you access to the combined learning of all four networks, without suffering the wrong turns and dead ends that we in Connecticut, the authors, and our colleagues in Cambridge, Iowa, and Ohio experienced along the way. Instructional rounds, as presented in these chapters, seems so logical, purposeful, and polished. It was never that way in the doing, which was fraught with anxiety and was much messier than the story told in these pages. Having been behind the curtain, I know there is no wizard.

Unlike many other educational how-to books currently on bookstore shelves, this one is not a cookbook of recipes for transforming schools and districts in five or six or seven steps. As the authors acknowledge, rounds in and of themselves will not raise student scores and will not help districts make adequate yearly progress to meet the provisions of the No Child Left Behind legislation. If rounds is going to lead to changes in teaching and learning, it cannot be another initiative, activity, or program imposed on superintendents, principals, and teachers. The power of rounds will only be realized when and if rounds becomes embedded in the actual work of the district. Only if rounds develops a collaborative, inquiry-based culture that shatters the norms of isolation and autonomy and if it leads to the establishment of an "educational practice" that trumps the notion of teaching as an art, a craft, or a style will rounds transform teaching and learning.

While rounds as a tool for systemic instructional improvement may seem a daunting prospect, Liz City, Richard Elmore, Sarah Fiarman, and Lee Teitel take us systematically through the process of planning, organizing, facilitating, implementing, and reflecting on rounds. *Instructional Rounds in Education* is chock full of concrete examples from the four networks that served as the petri dishes for this work. The practice of instructional rounds is demystified and made public, so that practitioners at every level, from chief state school officers to classroom teachers to coaches in school support organizations, can understand the process and protocols, assess their utility, and adapt them to the practitioners' unique circumstances.

If American students are going to compete in this increasingly flat world and global economy, education professionals must develop a practice and significantly improve it. Our schools must become places where both adults and students are continuously learning. *Instructional Rounds in Education* can assist educational practitioners in establishing and conducting rounds that exemplify a real community of practice, one in which teachers, principals, and superintendents collaborate in looking at student work, work together in solving instructional issues, and devise interventions for students who need extra attention. We owe that kind of fundamental change in teaching and learning to all the children in our schools.

In closing, I would be remiss if I did not recognize the contributions made by my colleagues at the Connecticut Center for School Change, whose probing questions and thoughtful suggestions enable us to continuously improve our practice. My deepest appreciation goes to all the superintendents who participated in the network over the past eight years. They are the instructional leaders on the front lines, and their commitment to improving teaching and learning continues to inspire me and give me hope for the future of public education. It is an honor to have worked with and for them.

Andrew Lachman
Executive Director, Connecticut Center
for Social Change

ACKNOWLEDGMENTS

We are deeply indebted to the networks of school and district leaders with whom we've worked and whose good ideas pepper these pages: the Cambridge Leadership Network, the Connecticut Superintendents' Network, the Iowa Leadership Academy Superintendents' Network, and the Ohio Leadership Collaborative. Their thoughtful participation and engagement helped develop the ideas that we share in this book. Each time a network member invested in the process by asking a question, expressing a concern, or sharing a suggestion (many, many great suggestions!), we learned ways to improve the process. We sincerely thank all of the network participants for their commitment to learning—their own learning, as well as that of the children and the adults in their schools and systems.

While the names of the network educators are too numerous to include here, a few have gone above and beyond to support their colleagues' learning as well as our own. These include those who boldly spearheaded the rounds efforts in each site, finding the time and means to sponsor a significant commitment to professional development: Andrew Lachman, Jane Tedder, and Steven Wlodarczyk in Connecticut, Tom Fowler-Finn and Carolyn Turk in Cambridge, Marilyn Troyer and Adrian Allison in Ohio, and Glenn Pelecky and Bonnie Boothroy in Iowa. Their vision for what the networks could bring to their settings continually held us and the network participants to a high standard.

Additionally, we thank the "Think Tank" members in Cambridge and Ohio. Each month, they volunteered their precious time to help shape the network for their peers. Conversations with these dedicated, wise leaders helped improve our own practice and helped push the work forward in each of these networks. They are: Bernie Burchett, Marcia Cussen, Michele Evans-Gardell, Christine Fowler-Mack, Mike Grote, Rob Kearns, Tom Milord, Sally Oldham, Jim Salzman, and Debbie Tully in Ohio; Barbara Boyle, Carole Learned-Miller, Maryann MacDonald, Nancy McLaughlin, Joe Petner, Damon Smith, and Carolyn Turk in Cambridge.

We thank our colleagues who took time from their busy schedules to read early drafts of chapters. They provided helpful feedback and equally helpful prodding to finish the book so they could use it in their own networks. They are: Jennifer Bennett, Bonnie Boothroy, Tom DelPrete, Tom Fowler-Finn, Andrew Lachman, Joe Micheller, Glenn Pelecky, Stefanie Reinhorn, Jim Salzman, and Carolyn Turk.

The wonderful team at Harvard Education Press shows that it's possible to have efficiency, quality, warmth, and a focus on influencing children's lives all at the same time. Special thanks to Caroline Chauncey and to the anonymous reviewers whose thoughtful comments helped us shape and reshape the book.

We would also like to acknowledge each other. We are big believers that you learn to do the work by doing the work, and we have certainly learned what it means to collaborate, challenge ideas, and form deep collegial relationships grounded in practice through the ongoing process of developing, refining, and writing about instructional rounds. On a title page, names must appear in some kind of sequence; in this case, ours are alphabetical and the authorship is equally shared. We're grateful to have had the opportunity to work with and learn from each other.

Finally, we thank our families who put up with too much travel and too many late meetings, and who provide the love and support that make us always look forward to coming home.

Why Professional Networks? Why Rounds? Why Practice?

Pierce Middle School is stuck. Despite the best efforts of its leadership and teaching staff, Pierce's results on the statewide test have leveled off, or slightly declined, after two years of more or less steady improvement. Pierce's staff feels the urgency of the situation. There is no question about their commitment to improved student learning. They feel they are working at the limit of their current knowledge and skill. The school district's leadership is equally concerned, since they were relying on Pierce to serve as a model for their systemwide improvement strategy. Now it's not clear what they will do. Maybe it's just a temporary glitch in the test scores. But maybe it's something more fundamental. Pierce's leadership team and the district leadership team huddle in a conference room at the central office trying to figure out what to do next. [1]

This scene, or something like it, occurs regularly in school systems across the country—educators with the best of intentions huddle down in conference rooms, looking at student performance data, trying to figure out what to do next in a school that seems to have outrun its knowledge of how to improve teaching and learning. In our work consulting with districts and schools on improvement, we routinely see this problem and others like it. In the typical case, teachers are working against the limits of their current knowledge about how to connect with students around content. School leaders are doing what they know how to do. District administrators are trying to send the right combination of signals of pressure and support to teachers and administrators, hoping that they will get it right.

Just as typically, in situations like this one, none of the parties to the discussion about what to do at Pierce *has any idea of what would solve Pierce's performance problem.* Each of the educators comes to the meeting with a set of impressions about what instructional practice looks like at Pierce. Each has a budding diagnosis about what might be going on at Pierce to explain its problem, but, just as likely, each has his or her own idea about what instruction looks like at Pierce and what it would have to look like in order to solve Pierce's problem.

American schools are under increasing pressure to produce better results than they have ever produced. No Child Left Behind has set a goal of 100 percent proficiency by 2014, and legislation is not the only source of pressure. A high school diploma is no longer a reliable ticket to a decent living. In an era of computers and instant access to information, problem solving, teamwork, and communication skills are essential for personal and national success. Most schools are falling far short of the 100 percent proficiency goal, and international assessments show us that American schools are at best in the middle of the pack among our peers in level of achievement. The problem is not that schools are worse than they used to be. In fact, according to the National Assessment of Educational Progress (NAEP), average scores in reading and math are higher than they were thirty years ago. The problem is not that educators aren't working hard. Walk into any school in America, and you will see adults who care deeply about their students and are doing the best they can every day to help students learn. The challenge is that we are asking schools to do something they have never done before—educate all students to high levels—and we don't know how to do that in every classroom for every child.

There are pockets of excellence throughout our schools and school systems. The students lucky enough to be in the pockets are well prepared to make a good life for themselves and for their community. The students left out of the pockets are not so fortunate. That these students tend to be students of color and living in poverty is a sad, unacceptable description of our past and present, but does not have to describe our future. Our challenge is to bring those pockets of excellence to scale—to provide for all what our systems currently provide for some.

In the United States, we have more variation in student achievement than do almost all of our international peers, and it matters tremendously which classroom students are in. This is no surprise, given the traditional teaching norms of autonomy and isolation. It is clear that closed classroom doors will not help us educate all students to high levels. It is also clear that what happens in classrooms matters for student learning and that we can do more together than we can do individually to improve learning and teaching. However, not all forms of professional development and collaboration are created equal. Slowly, the image of the teacher behind the closed classroom door is giving way to an image of an open door, but many educators are not sure what to look for when they open the door and what to do with what they see.

Repeatedly, district and school practitioners tell us that one of the greatest barriers to school improvement is the lack of an agreed-upon definition of what high-quality instruction looks like. Without some understanding of what instruction at Pierce actually looks like and some agreement about what it would have to look like to achieve the kind of student learning that Pierce is trying to achieve, the meeting at the central office is not likely to produce much. Yet, time and again, educators meet to try to solve instructional problems without a common understanding of what they are trying to achieve in the classroom.

Our work in schools is about bridging this knowledge gap between educators and their practice. The *rounds process* is an explicit practice that is designed to bring discussions of instruction directly into the process of school improvement. By *practice*, we mean something quite specific. We mean a set of protocols and processes for observing, analyzing, discussing, and understanding instruction that can be used to improve student learning at scale. The practice works because it creates a common discipline and focus among practitioners with a common purpose and set of problems.

The rounds process is an adaptation and extension of the medical rounds model, which is used routinely in medical schools and teaching hospitals to develop the diagnostic and treatment practice of physicians. There are several versions of medical rounds, but in the most commonly used versions, groups of medical interns, residents, and supervising or attending physicians visit patients, observe and discuss the evidence for diagnoses, and, after a thorough analysis of the evidence, discuss possible treatments. The medical rounds process is the major way in which physicians develop their knowledge of practice and, more importantly, the major way in which the profession builds and propagates its norms of practice.[2] The rounds model embodies a specific set of ideas about how practitioners work together to solve common problems and to improve their practice. In the education context, we call this practice *instructional rounds*, or *rounds* for short.

Educators do, of course, have practices. That is, each teacher, principal, curriculum coach, and system-level administrator has, implicitly or explicitly, some set of "customary, habitual, or expected" ways of doing work. What educators don't have are explicitly *shared* practices, which is what distinguishes educators from other professionals. It is this idea of shared practice that is at the core of instructional rounds. The basic idea is to put all educators—principals and central office administrators as well as teachers—into a common practice disciplined by protocols and routines and organized around the core functions of schooling in order to create common language, ways of seeing, and a shared practice of improvement.

[handwritten margin note: another def. of rounds]

WHAT ROUNDS IS—AND ISN'T

Instructional rounds sits at the intersection of three current popular approaches to the improvement of teaching and learning—walkthroughs, networks, and district improvement strategies.

Since what goes on in classrooms is at the heart of instructional improvement, a key part of developing an improvement practice is observation. We are not alone in attending to this. Dozens of other approaches use various forms of classroom observation, calling them walkthroughs, learning walks, classroom visitations, peer (or administrative) observations, and more. A wide range of activities goes under the broad *walkthrough* umbrella—some activities supportive of good instruction, others punitive and uninformed. Some focus attention on instruction and bring together educators in ways that lead to improvement; others are technical, compliance driven, cursory (referred to derisively by teachers as "drive-bys"), and harshly evaluative.

Unfortunately, the practice of walkthroughs has become corrupted in many ways by confounding it with the supervision and evaluation of teachers. The purpose of some walkthroughs has been to identify deficiencies in classroom practice and to "fix" teachers who manifest these deficiencies. In many instances, judgments about what needs fixing are made on the basis of simplistic checklists that have little or nothing to do with the direct experience of teachers in their classrooms. Groups of administrators descend on classrooms with clipboards and checklists, caucus briefly in the hallway, and then deliver a set of simplistic messages about what needs fixing. This kind of practice is both antithetical to the purposes of instructional rounds and profoundly antiprofessional. The idea behind instructional rounds is that *everyone* involved is working on their practice, *everyone* is obliged to be knowledgeable about the common task of instructional improvement, and *everyone's* practice should be subject to scrutiny, critique, and improvement.

Networks are also a common idea in educational improvement circles. It seems as if you cannot turn around in a school or district with an improvement agenda without bumping into some kind of network—a professional learning community, a critical friends group, or a teacher or principal study group. Some are within districts or within schools, and some cut across districts, perhaps organized for subject-area teachers or a particular type of administrator. Some approaches in the network category are well thought-out, well implemented, and tied to improving practice, but many are not. In some settings, they are simply new labels for meetings that are dysfunctional or disconnected from instructional improvement, or both. In rounds networks, colleagues (possibly sharing the same role, like superintendents, or possibly in mixed roles, like superintendents, central office personnel, teachers union leaders, professional developers, principals, and teachers) gather regularly to engage in and develop the practice of rounds together, over time developing a community of practice that supports their improvement work.

Our goal is to support systems of instructional improvement at scale, not just isolated pockets of good teaching in the midst of mediocrity. Consequently, a key part of the instructional rounds practice connects the classroom observations of the rounds model to the larger context of the system's improvement strategy. It is a rare school system that doesn't have an improvement plan, but they range widely in quality, focus, and usefulness. Some are dynamic and are used to drive instruction and align operations; others are exercises that end up summarized in several volumes that sit on the superintendent's shelf. Some plans are collections of activities, not framed around a central idea or focus, or even a hypothesis about what actions will logically lead to desired improvements.

Having an improvement strategy, at some stage of development, is a precondition for the effective use of instructional rounds. The process of rounds requires participants to focus on a common problem of practice that cuts across all levels of the system. It is difficult to focus in a productive way on which problem to solve if you don't have a strategy to start with. The more developed the strategy, the more you are likely to benefit from the practice of rounds. Rounds draws on and contributes to a system's strategy. Virtually all the districts we have worked with have markedly changed their improvement strategies over the course of their work with us, building on the knowledge and shared vision of teaching and learning they have developed through the use of instructional rounds. Our experience with rounds has been primarily at the district level, building a practice among system-level and school-level leadership teams around instructional improvement. The same practice could be used in a single school, a department in a high school, or a network of autonomous schools with a mutual interest in improvement.

Rounds is a special kind of walkthrough, a special kind of network, and a special kind of improvement strategy integrated into one practice.

A Picture of Rounds

Rounds is a four-step process: identifying a problem of practice, observing, debriefing, and focusing on the next level of work. While this process is described in much greater detail later in the book (see chapters 5 and 6, in particular), we offer a summary here to give you a picture of what it looks like.

A network convenes in a school for a rounds visit hosted by a member or members of the network (e.g., principal or superintendent). The focus of the visit is a *problem of practice*, the specific problem of instructional improvement that the school and the school system are wrestling with and would like the network's feedback on. The problem of practice might be something like this: *In reading and writing, our students seem to be doing relatively well on decoding, vocabulary, and simple writing tasks, but they are not doing as well as we had hoped on comprehension and open-response tasks. Teachers have begun using a workshop method to work with smaller groups of students, but there is no consistency in what happens in those small groups.*

The network divides into smaller groups that visit a *rotation* of four or five classrooms for approximately twenty minutes each. In classrooms, network participants write down what they see and hear, gathering descriptive evidence related to the problem of practice. After completing classroom observations, the entire group assembles in a common location for a debriefing. In the debrief, participants work through a process of description, analysis, and prediction. Individual participants share their observations in groups, building a body of evidence about what they saw going on in classrooms and how it seemed to bear on the problem of practice. The evidence might be visible in the form of flip-chart sheets arrayed on the walls of the school library and covered with sticky notes that capture the things that individuals saw going on. The groups then analyze the evidence for patterns and look at how what they have seen explains, or doesn't explain, the observable student performance in the school. Finally, the network discusses the *next level of work*, recommendations for the school and system to make progress on the problem of practice.

The Pierce debriefing, for example, might have surfaced a common issue that we see routinely in schools, which is that the broader purposes of the literacy strategy are not evident in the actual work that students are being asked to do. So, for example, we might see curriculum guidance that presupposes students were being asked to produce significant amounts of text in classrooms, but the actual work that students are observed doing might be relatively short answer responses to closed-end questions. From this set of observations might come a suggestion for the next level of work. For example, administrators and coaches might familiarize themselves with the practices that are associated with higher-level work and increase their focus on these practices in professional development. Another suggestion might be that in their group sessions, teacher teams focus more specifically on evidence of student work that represents higher-level literacy.

A network meeting might also include professional development to deepen network members' knowledge and skill related to the problem of practice (e.g., reading an article about literacy). Some networks choose a common focus for a sustained period, like higher-order thinking skills or math, examining problems of practice and building their expertise in the focal area. Over time, the network rotates through the schools or systems of all the network members, developing a shared understanding of learning and teaching, as well as a common practice together, and thus meeting both purposes of rounds: to build the knowledge and skills of the group and to provide helpful feedback and suggestions of support for the host school.

ROUNDS AS AN ORGANIZATIONAL PROCESS

As the Pierce example suggests, the advent of schools' increased accountability for student performance has resulted in increased pressure for schools to engage in explicit schoolwide planning. Most schools have received and understood the message that they are supposed to be concerned about student learning and performance, and most educators have now accepted that it is part of their responsibility to pay attention to measurable student outcomes. But the exact process by which this is supposed to occur is often quite fuzzy. It is now fairly typical for principals, coaches, and professional developers to periodically enter teachers' classrooms for various purposes. It is not typical for these various parties to have a common definition of what they are looking for. In the absence of such an agreement, teachers receive conflicting signals about what they are supposed to be doing, and they are forced to choose between competing ideas about what constitutes good practice, if they receive any feedback at all.

In this context, the rounds model brings a set of practices that can be used by schools and school systems to develop a common understanding of the work of instructional practice. It forces multiple actors, with often quite different interests and ideas, to begin the difficult process of forming a coherent view of what constitutes powerful teaching and learning in classrooms. It also forces a certain discipline around the relationship between teachers and those whose job it is to support and supervise them. The rounds process says, in effect, that teachers should be able to operate under coherent guidance and support for their teaching, and that those who purport to supervise and support teachers have an obligation to work out their differences in ways that lead to a coherent result in the classroom.

The rounds process also takes head-on the traditional norms around the privacy of teaching. Effective schools are coherent learning environments for adults and students. Coherence means that the adults agree on what they are trying to accomplish with students and that the adults are consistent from classroom to classroom in their expectations for what students are expected to learn. Coherent learning environments cannot exist in incoherent organizations. So the rounds model presupposes that a condition of school improvement is opening up the classroom to more or less routine interaction between teachers, administrators, and support personnel, and the development of a common language for doing the work. Teachers are often justifiably skeptical about opening up their classrooms to outsiders, because it often results in conflicting and vague advice that has little practical value to them or their students. Hence, the rounds process operates on the principle that challenges to the norm of privacy in teaching should be accompanied by a reciprocal obligation to provide coherent and useful guidance and support for instructional practice.

ROUNDS AS A LEARNING PROCESS

School improvement is, in essence, a knowledge-intensive activity. Teachers and administrators don't have all their best ideas locked away in closets, waiting for the accountability system to hammer them with bad news and cause them to bring these ideas out into the light of day. Most educators are working, for better or for worse, at, or very near, the limit of their existing knowledge and skill. You don't improve schools by giving them bad news about their performance. You improve schools by using information about student learning, from multiple sources, to find the most promising instructional problems to work on, and then systematically developing with teachers and administrators the knowledge and skill necessary to solve those problems. Typically, what's happening in a school like Pierce is that the school is doing a reasonably good job of what it is trying to do—it is just continuing to work on a problem it has already solved, and hasn't moved on to the next problem, which is the one that is getting in the way of its improved performance. To use the medical analogy, Pierce is doing a good job of curing a disorder that it has already cured, and it needs to diagnose and respond to the next disorder to improve the school's performance. In order to make this transition from the problem we have already solved to the *next* problem we need to solve, we need much more detailed knowledge of what is going on at Pierce than we currently have, and we need to have a common understanding of which problem we are going to work on next.

The advent of accountability has caused many school systems to increase their instructional support and professional development. It is now the rare school system that doesn't provide at least some support for teachers, organized around the system's current instructional priorities. In addition, accountability has put increasing pressure on school administrators to at least look as if they are actively managing instruction in their buildings. Often, this takes the form of system-level expectations that principals will spend a certain amount of time in classrooms.

In many cases, like Pierce, where the system has bet a substantial amount of its resources on the expectation of improvement, we are likely to see a number of parties working in a school. Consequently, school people are likely to be exposed to various experts' views on what they should be doing. It is important to understand that these well-intentioned activities rarely lead to systematic improvement in instructional practice and student learning. Virtually all the low-performing schools we work with are overwhelmed with people from multiple sectors and multiple levels of government telling them what to do. The problem is not that the schools don't have access to knowledge. The problem is that they don't have a process for translating that knowledge systematically into practice. The knowledge and support that most schools receive fall on an organization that is weakly equipped to use these offerings, because it doesn't have the *internal structures, processes, and norms* that are necessary to pick up the knowledge and deploy it in classrooms. Knowledge doesn't stick in such schools, because they don't have the receptors in the organization to pick it up and use it.

The model of learning that is embodied in the rounds process, which we develop more fully in chapter 8, puts educators in the position of having to actively construct their own knowledge of effective instructional practice and to develop, among colleagues who have to work together on school improvement, a shared understanding of what they mean by effective instruction. The process of active construction helps educators articulate and refine their own theories about how to support learning and builds their capacity to both use and generate knowledge. There is, unapologetically, a certain "constructivist" bias in the rounds process. When we work with people, we specifically avoid giving them "answers" to the most pressing problems they face, because to give "answers" would be to transfer the responsibility for learning from them to us.

The rounds process, then, is about creating and modeling a specific set of ideas about how schools and systems can learn from their own practices, develop a more acute understanding of the *next* problem they need to solve, and take control of their own learning in ways that are more likely to lead to sustained improvement over time.

ROUNDS AS A CULTURE-BUILDING PROCESS

Language is culture. Culture is language. One of the things we have learned from the medical profession about the improvement of practice is that how people talk to each other about what they are doing is an important determinant of whether they are able to learn from their practice. That is, the language that physicians use to talk about their practice embodies a set of cultural expectations about the relationship between the evidence they see in the diagnostic process, the protocols they use to discover the meaning of diagnostic information, and the ways in which they develop a shared understanding of what to do for patients.[3] The isolated culture of schools works against shared conceptions of problems and practices. The rounds process is designed to develop a language and a culture for breaking down the isolation of teachers' practice.

The rounds process requires educators to engage in unfamiliar behaviors. Participants must use language in a different way than they are accustomed to using it. People have to interact with each other in ways that are often at odds with the prevailing collegial culture of schools. And rounds requires sustained interaction around the details of instructional practice in ways that are seldom part of the daily routines of schooling. The initial awkwardness and discomfort these practices generate is due to the challenge that the rounds process places on the established culture of instructional practice, using language and interaction as the medium of exchange. If the process did not result in awkwardness and disequilibrium, it would not effect any significant cultural transformation.

An example of this discomfort comes from a typical pattern in the early stages of our work with practitioners. Not surprisingly, participants are often drawn to "student engagement" in their early observations. So it is typical to hear participants say in debriefing and analysis sessions that they saw students who were "highly engaged" or "disengaged." When we push them for evidence of what they would call student engagement—that is, what did they actually see that led them to the judgment that students were engaged or disengaged?—it turns out that participants focus on five or six types of evidence, often with contradictory definitions of engagement. Some people focus on whether students are paying attention to the teacher, some on whether the students are actively doing what the teacher has asked them to do, some on whether the students seem to understand what they are expected to do, some on whether students seem to like what they are doing, and so forth. In ordinary discourse in schools, the term *student engagement* would be allowed to pass through the discussion with no expectation of a common definition. So if the conclusion of the observation was that teachers ought to stimulate student engagement, teachers might carry away any of five or six ideas about what that meant, and would probably choose the one definition that is closest to what they are already doing. The advice that participants would give to teachers about engagement would have a similarly diffuse and contradictory quality. When we hold participants to the possible contradictions and ambiguities of how they are using the language around student engagement, we create a considerable amount of discomfort, but over time, they learn that the language they use has an important impact on the culture they are creating.

ROUNDS AS A POLITICAL PROCESS

At this particular juncture in the history of American education, it is controversial to argue that teaching is a profession that requires high levels of knowledge and skill and that, like any profession, teachers are required to continue to develop their knowledge and skill actively over the course their careers. The nineteenth-century idea that teaching is relatively low-skill work that can be performed by anyone with a nodding familiarity with content and an affinity for children is alive and well in the policy discourse of the present reform period. Just the suggestion that teaching and school leadership require a deep knowledge of instructional practice and a grounding in professional protocols for bringing knowledge into practice is likely to incite raised eyebrows on the part of many critics of American education. Presently, policy makers and critics lack much understanding of the actual knowledge and skill requirements of what they are asking educators to do. Educators are relatively powerless in this discussion because they are, as a group, active co-conspirators in the trivialization of educational expertise. School organization and culture, for the most part, do not exemplify a professional work environment as the broader society understands it.

In this context, then, it is likely to be controversial to argue that educators should have a *practice* of school improvement, that this practice should be framed around protocols and norms of professional discourse, and that people should be required to demonstrate knowledge of and proficiency in the practice in order to continue their employment as educators. Also likely to be controversial, both within and outside the education sector, is the observation that the traditional culture of atomized teaching is antithetical both to school improvement and to the professionalization of teaching. The idea that successful teachers are born, not made, and that "good teaching" is a gift, not a skill acquired by hard work and persistence over an entire career, is alive and well in American society and culture.

Any practice that tries to solidify and consolidate professional expertise around teaching and the organizational conditions that support it is likely to generate political controversy. Any efforts to raise the professional stature of teaching, and education in general, are likely to activate traditional cultural stereotypes of teachers and teaching and to incite discomfort among people who resist raising the occupational status of teachers for practical and ideological reasons. Like any idea that attempts to alter the distribution of knowledge and authority in society, the rounds process is not a politically neutral idea. It carries with it a certain set of assumptions about the value of the knowledge that educators bring to their work, and it consolidates that knowledge in ways that increase the professional authority of educators.

It will become evident as this book progresses that the practice summarized here is actually quite complex in action and requires sustained attention and effort to be done well. The level of knowledge and skill that participants manifest in the early stages of this practice is usually not a thing of beauty. But we now know from experience that people get better and better at the work over time. Educators report that the rounds work increases their acuity and sophistication around instructional issues and builds a strong set of collegial relationships with a common language and common set of concerns.

Great! good!

SOME BACKGROUND ON US AND OUR NETWORKS

Each of us came to the rounds process from a different point of departure, stimulated by a common interest in how to give educators more influence and control over the conditions of their work and a more powerful practice around student learning in classrooms. Richard Elmore came to the work via a stimulating partnership several years ago with Penelope Peterson and Sarah McCarthey around a book about the relationship between teaching practice and school organization.[4] This initial interest stimulated a longer-term focus on how schools make instructional decisions and how they decide to whom and for what they are accountable in the current reform environment. He subsequently helped launch the first rounds network in Connecticut and drew the rest of the authors into the practice.

Sarah Fiarman came to the work as an elementary school teacher with a strong interest in developing communities of practice and experience as a consultant and professional developer around quality instruction. Lee Teitel has a long-term interest in leadership practice in schools and school systems and has been a consultant and professional developer in leadership development programs at the local, state, and national levels. Elizabeth City is an experienced teacher, principal, and consultant with an interest in supporting educators to improve learning for every student.

Our work with instructional rounds has taken place in four types of networks, and we share examples from the networks throughout the book. Elmore and Teitel have worked on the development of the rounds model in the Connecticut Superintendents' Network, organized by the Connecticut Center for School Change. The first cohort of the Connecticut Superintendents' Network began in 2001, with a second cohort added in 2005. Each cohort includes about twelve superintendents representing geographically and demographically diverse districts.

Elmore, Fiarman, and City worked together on the development of a rounds model for school and system-level administrators in Cambridge, Massachusetts. The Cambridge Leadership Network began in 2005 and involves about thirty people—all the principals in the district, the high school deans of instruction, the president of the teachers union, and several central office staff, including the superintendent and the deputy superintendent. This was designed and implemented as a turnkey initiative, a model of improvement that principals and system-level administrators could take over and build on without outside facilitation at the end of a two-year cycle.

Together, Elmore, Fiarman, Teitel, and City are currently supporting the development of rounds models in Ohio and Iowa at the state and regional levels.[5] The Ohio Leadership Collaborative is a team-based network begun in 2007. It combines the cross-district features of the Connecticut model and several key in-district aspects of Cambridge. The network began with five urban districts, each with a five-person team—in most cases made up of the superintendent, the chief academic officer, union leadership, a principal, and a teacher. Currently, there are four participating districts (one district left the network as a result of significant central office turnover) with approximately ten-person teams. State department of education personnel also participate, as do facilitators who are learning the practice in order to support each district in its subsequent internal rounds ramp-up. During the first year, the primary focus was on learning the rounds practice by conducting visits in each of the five participating districts. During the second year, each district has begun to develop and implement its own in-district rounds process with school teams. The Iowa Leadership Academy Superintendents' Network builds on an existing organizational structure of regional superintendent groups. The first network was started in 2008 in Area Education Agency 9 (AEA 9) with an explicit scale-up agenda of launching superintendents' networks throughout the state in early 2009. The networks are to be supported by facilitators and superintendents who have learned the practice with AEA 9.

This is a book, in others words, about practice written out of the experience of working with practitioners and taking an initial set of ideas through successive stages of development, clarification, experimentation, and documentation. In the book, we describe the rounds approach to large-scale instructional improvement that we have helped initiate in four states, affecting more than one hundred districts and over one thousand schools.

A BRIEF OVERVIEW OF THE BOOK

This book is intended to help educators at all levels of school systems, as well as the partners and policy makers who support them, to improve learning and teaching in every classroom. We've divided the book into three sections that explain both the theory and the practice of rounds: Building Blocks; Doing Rounds; and

Rounds and Systemic Improvement. Each chapter begins with a vignette based on our rounds experience and concludes with a few key takeaway points.

Building Blocks

While much of the understanding that comes through rounds is developed by engaging in the practice, there are two pieces of knowledge that form a foundation from which participants build their understanding over time: (1) the instructional core and (2) theory of action. Chapter 1 includes a description of the instructional core (teachers and students working together in the presence of content) and seven principles that connect the instructional core to improvement at scale. Focusing educators' attention on the instructional core and their role in it is a prime function of instructional rounds.

Chapter 2 defines theory of action as a clearly articulated, testable hypothesis about cause and effect. This hypothesis undergirds a district's improvement strategy—"if we do X activity or approach, then we are likely to get Y outcome." Understanding theory of action helps educators articulate both how they think instructional rounds will lead to intended outcomes and how rounds connects with the larger district strategy. In our work, we find that explicitly linking action with intended outcomes is a critical component of a coherent improvement strategy.

These chapters serve as a primer in the development of a rounds network. They help a group develop a common understanding of the basic terms and concepts central to the rounds practice.

Doing Rounds

This section shows the whole process of rounds, from initial start-up into classrooms to the postobservation debriefing. Chapter 3 answers many of the questions that arise when educators are forming instructional rounds networks. These questions include the following: Who should be involved? How big should the network be? What kinds of resources, including time, are needed? What kinds of commitments and norms should the network have? How do you get buy-in from participants? What needs to be established from the beginning, and what can the network define over time? The chapter also shares examples from our experience of networks that have had different answers to these questions.

Since what goes on in classrooms is at the heart of instructional improvement, a key part of developing an improvement practice is observation—learning to see what is going on in classrooms. Chapter 4 describes how to prepare for instructional rounds, including developing the discipline of seeing and describing at a fine-grained level what is happening in classrooms. In our experience, educators tend to leap quickly to inference and judgment (e.g., "Students were really engaged" or "That was a great lesson!"), which impedes their ability to assemble and analyze a body of evidence as a foundation of improvement. This chapter shows why description matters as well as how to unlearn judgmental habits and learn descriptive habits.

Chapters 5 and 6 describe the four steps of the rounds process: defining a problem of practice, observing practice, debriefing , and focusing on the next level of work. Chapter 5 describes how to define a helpful problem of practice and includes nuts and bolts like how many classrooms to visit for how long and what to do and not do while in classrooms. Chapter 6 includes protocols for debriefing classroom observations and moving from piles of evidence to a narrow focus on what the host school and district might do next to improve learning and teaching.

Chapter 7 looks behind the scenes at the rounds process, with particular attention to the role of facilitators. While it takes some time to build network participants' skill at observation, analysis, and the next level of work, it's possible to accelerate the pace of the network's learning and application of that learning. The chapter examines how facilitators can support and accelerate the group's learning by modeling the work, responding to local circumstances, moving forward with a coherent agenda, and cultivating the network. While this chapter is aimed directly at facilitators, we recommend that everyone read it since we are strong believers in the collective nature of rounds. Understanding the whole process helps everyone take responsibility for improving it along the way.

Rounds and Systemic Improvement

The final section of the book describes the assumptions and actions that take rounds from merely an interesting activity to a practice with systemic impact. Chapter 8 describes the learning theory that undergirds the rounds process, including our theory of action for how rounds leads to systemic improvement. This discussion appears at this point in the book because we have found that the theory makes more sense when you have a picture of the practice. Thus, the learning theory offers a bridge between the practice shown in the "Doing Rounds" section and the systemic improvement discussed in chapter 9.

Chapter 9 describes how the rounds practice informs, and is informed by, a system's improvement strategy. The chapter shows what happens beyond a rounds visit, including examples from our experience of schools and districts engaging in an iterative process: Problems of practice are drawn from improvement strategies; the rounds process focuses on those problems of practice; and then the evidence, analysis, and dialogue from the rounds process inform both short- and longer-term plans for improvement at scale.

The appendix includes sample materials from our instructional rounds work. We also include a Further Reading and Resources section at the back of the book to suggest texts to further support learning through the rounds process.

We recommend reading the book one time in sequence, and then rereading chapters once you begin to engage in the work of rounds. The experience of rounds will help you know which chapters you want to revisit. (Need ideas for how to stay in the descriptive mode? See chapter 4. Ready to start drafting a theory of action? See chapter 2. Wondering how facilitators cultivate trust? See chapter 7.) You may be tempted to skip right to chapters 5 and 6, read the details of the rounds practice, and then dive into doing instructional rounds. Though there is much to be said for doing the work, we're confident that you'll have better success linking rounds to systemic improvement if you read all the chapters before you begin rounds. And then, by all means, dive in.

PART 1

Building Blocks

CHAPTER 1

The Instructional Core

The Kendall School, a K–8 school in a suburban neighborhood, is struggling with its mathematics curriculum. The district has adopted a new math curriculum, keyed to the state content and performance standards, and the Kendall School is into its second full year of implementation. It is clear not only that the curriculum is not improving math performance—scores have actually declined in a few classrooms—but also that teachers are struggling with the new content. Parents are beginning to express frustration because they don't understand the homework that students are bringing home and the math problems in the homework don't look anything like the math that they studied when they were in school. Pat Granger, the principal of Kendall, is starting to field complaints from both teachers and parents about the state of math instruction.

The district math coordinator and the professional development consultant whom the district has hired have a different view. "The problem, as far as I'm concerned," the math coordinator says, "is that this is not just a change in content—it is a change in the whole way we think about math in the classroom. It requires teachers to put much more control in the hands of students; it requires students to think about the mathematical ideas, not just the procedures; and it requires a significantly higher level of mathematical knowledge than teachers have been expected to have."

Granger says, "We thought we were adopting a curriculum, and it turns out, we've adopted a monster. This thing has set off a whole range of issues we're not very well prepared to deal with."

What's happening at the Kendall School is a version of what happens whenever a school or system undertakes an instructional change that is well outside the existing knowledge and skill set of students, teachers, and administrators. Students are unfamiliar with the new classroom demands and, for the most part, don't understand why content that was familiar to them in the past now seems strange and unfamiliar. Teachers find their established ways of teaching disrupted and are confronted with classroom management and pedagogy issues for which they may have only minimal preparation. Administrators are faced not just with responding to teachers' expressions of uncertainty, but also the reverberations of this uncertainty through students and their parents. What's going on here is that the system has adopted a *disruptive technology*—a curriculum and a set of pedagogical practices that require people to think and act differently than they have in the past.[1] The sources of uncertainty in this disruptive technology are rooted in the relationship between the teacher and the student in the presence of content—the instructional core (figure 1.1). Making meaningful and productive changes in instructional practice requires us to confront how they upset and, in some sense, reprogram our past ways of doing things. The success of the new math curriculum at Kendall depends on understanding exactly what has to change in the instructional core for the new curriculum to deliver on its promise of higher learning of mathematics. The instructional core anchors the practice of rounds and any other school- or district-level instructional improvement process.

In its simplest terms, the instructional core is composed of the teacher and the student in the presence of content. In the work of the philosopher of education,

FIGURE 1.1   THE INSTRUCTIONAL CORE

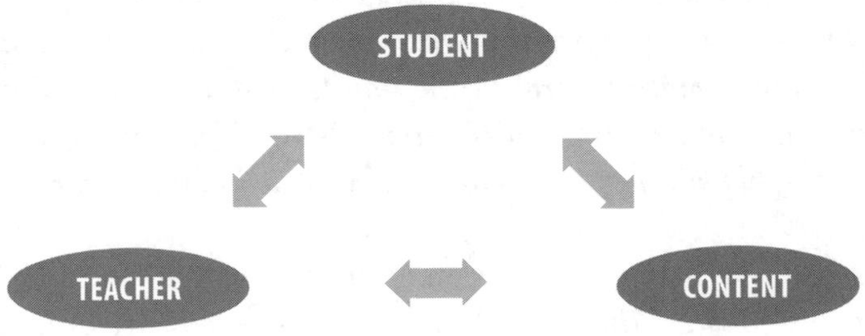

FIGURE 1.2   SEVEN PRINCIPLES OF THE INSTRUCTIONAL CORE

1. Increases in student learning occur only as a consequence of improvements in the level of content, teachers' knowledge and skill, and student engagement.

2. If you change any single element of the instructional core, you have to change the other two.

3. If you can't see it in the core, it's not there.

4. Task predicts performance.

5. The real accountability system is in the tasks that students are asked to do.

6. We learn to do the work by doing the work, *not* by telling other people to do the work, *not* by having done the work at some time in the past, and *not* by hiring experts who can act as proxies for our knowledge about how to do the work.

7. Description before analysis, analysis before prediction, prediction before evaluation.

David Hawkins, this is the "I" (the teacher), the "thou" (the student), and the "it" (the content).[2] As the Hawkins framework was developed and elaborated on by David Cohen and Deborah Ball, it is the *relationship* between the teacher, the student, and the content—*not* the qualities of any one of them by themselves—that determines the nature of instructional practice, and each corner of the instructional core has its own particular role and resources to bring to the instructional process.[3] In his seminal work on instructional practice, Walter Doyle locates the *instructional task* at the center of the instructional core.[4] Simply stated, the instructional task is the actual work that students are asked to do in the process of instruction—*not* what teachers *think* they are asking students to do, or what the official curriculum *says* that students are asked to do, but what they are *actually* asked to do. So, for example, in an "advanced" science class, if students are asked to memorize elements and their atomic structures, the actual task that the students are being asked to do is a memorization task, even though the teacher might think that because the material is difficult and the work is beyond what students in the "regular" science class are being asked to do, it is a higher-level task.

The model of the instructional core provides the basic framework for how to intervene in the instructional process so as to improve the quality and level of student learning. Seven principles guide our work with the instructional core (figure 1.2).

FIRST PRINCIPLE: *Increases in student learning occur only as a consequence of improvements in the level of content, teachers' knowledge and skill, and student engagement.*

There are only three ways to improve student learning at scale. The first is to increase the level of knowledge and skill that the teacher brings to the instructional process. The second is to increase the level and complexity of the content that students are asked to learn. And the third is to change the role of the student in the instructional process. That's it. If you are not doing one of these three things, you are not improving instruction and learning. Everything else is instrumental. That is, everything that's *not* in the instructional core can only affect student learning and performance by somehow influencing what goes on *inside* the core.

When educators think about "changing" instruction, they typically focus not on the instructional core, but on the various structures and processes that surround the core. They might choose, for example, to group students in a particular way because of a theory about how grouping will affect the relationship of the student and the teacher in the presence of content. But it is not the grouping practice that produces student learning. Rather, it is the change in the knowledge and skill that teachers bring to the practice, the type of content to which students gain access, and the role that students play in their own learning that determine what students will know and be able to do. If changes in grouping practices don't alter the core, then the likelihood they will affect student learning is remote.

What about content and performance standards? Standards only operate by influencing the level of the content that's actually being taught. Their effect in actual classrooms depends on whether there are materials that reflect the standards, whether teachers know how to teach what the materials and standards require, and whether students find the work that they are being asked to do worthwhile and engaging.

What about professional development? Professional development works, if it works at all, by influencing what teachers *do*, not by influencing what they think they ought to do or what the professional developers think teachers ought to do. The quality and impact of professional development depends on what teachers are being asked to learn, how they are learning it, and whether they can make the practices they are being asked to try work in their classrooms.

What about supervision, evaluation, and strong instructional leadership? Administrators' influence on the quality and effectiveness of classroom instruction is determined *not* by the leadership practices they manifest, but by the way those practices influence the knowledge and skill of teachers, the level of work in classrooms, and level of active learning by students. Much of what well-intentioned policy makers and administrators do in the name of school improvement never actually reaches the instructional core. Much of it doesn't even reach the classroom, much less inside the classroom. Our best ideas about policy and management don't *cause* student learning to increase. At the very best, when they are working well, they *create conditions* that influence what goes on inside the instructional core. The primary work of schooling occurs inside classrooms, *not* in the organizations and institutions that surround the classroom. Schools don't improve through political and managerial incantation; they improve through the complex and demanding work of teaching and learning.

SECOND PRINCIPLE: *If you change any single element of the instructional core, you have to change the other two to affect student learning.*

The second principle follows from the first. So, for example, if your improvement strategy begins with a curriculum solution—say, as at the Kendall School, the adoption of a new math curriculum—then you have to invest in the new knowledge and skill required of teachers to teach that curriculum if you expect it to contribute to new student learning. A failure to address teachers' knowledge and skill as part of a curriculum-based improvement strategy typically produces low-level teaching of high-level content, a situation we see with considerable frequency in American classrooms. We call this "knocking the corners off the grand piano to get it through the door." Teachers assign high-level text or complex problems and then structure student learning around familiar fill-in-the-blank worksheets. Or teachers walk students through a straight procedural explanation of how to find the answer, leaving the students in the role of recording what the teacher says, rather than actively thinking through the problems for themselves. If you invest in teacher professional development without a clear understanding of where you expect it to lead in terms of the actual content that students are expected to master, then you get random innovation across classrooms and the innovation has no systemwide or schoolwide impact on student learning.

If you raise the level of content *and* the knowledge and skill of teachers without changing the role of the student in the instructional process, you get another common situation in American classrooms: Teachers are doing all, or most, of the work,

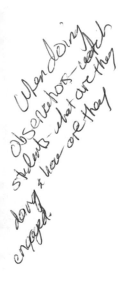

exercising considerable flair and control in the classroom, and students are sitting passively, watching the teacher perform. A common student question in these classrooms is, "Teacher, should I write this down?" If you raise the level of teachers' knowledge and skill in general pedagogy without anchoring it in content, you get high-level practice disconnected from a clear understanding of what students are actually learning, and from the specific issues that students have with specific cognitive tasks. This is what David Hawkins means when he says, "Without an it, there is no content for the context, no figure, no heat, but only an affair of mirrors confronting each other."[5]

We frequently hear educators talk about how well the lesson went, without reference to what students were actually doing and the visible evidence of what students actually knew as a consequence of the teaching. Mostly, the lesson has "gone well" when it has gone according to plan, without any specific reference to what students do or don't know as a consequence of the teaching. Intervening on any single axis of the instructional core means that you have to intervene on the other two to have a predictable effect on student learning.

If you invest in higher-level content *and* teacher knowledge and skill, but you neglect the role of the student in the instructional process, you get students (and parents) who, as at the Kendall School, don't understand the new roles and demands that they are expected to meet. Americans are much more comfortable talking about changing content and teaching than they are about changing the role of the student in instruction. We focus much more attention on textbook adoptions and curriculum alignment, for example, than we do on analyzing students' actual responses to the content, what motivates them to high levels of engagement with the content, and their actual role in the instructional process. In the more advanced strategies of improvement, we focus attention on helping teachers get familiar with new content and pedagogy, but we focus relatively little attention on what students are doing when they are actively engaged in learning what we think they should learn.

This is one big difference between American schools and schools in other countries. Here we spend a great deal of time worrying about *what* we're teaching and *how* it is being taught. In other places, people also spend a great deal of time worrying about *whether* students are actually interested in, actively engaged in, and able to explain how they the students think about what adults are trying to teach them. There are differences between elementary schools and secondary schools in the United States on this score. It is much more common, although still not the dominant practice, in U.S. elementary schools for teachers to pay attention to whether students are actually interested and engaged in learning. Most of the instruction we observe in secondary schools is about "delivering" the content and, most importantly, about deciding which students are smart and which are "deserving" of further attainment. The culture of American schools, in its deep structure, is very teacher-centric. You only see the magnitude of this when you step outside the culture. We tend to focus more on what the teacher is doing in front of the classroom than we do on the work that is actually on top of the student's desk. More about this later.

The instructional core provides a heuristic for assessing the likelihood that any systemic improvement strategy, or any particular change in policy or practice, will result in any real improvement in student learning:

- How will this affect teachers' knowledge and skills?
- How will this affect the level of content in classrooms?
- How will this affect the role of the student in the instructional process?
- How will this affect the relationship between the teacher, the student, and content?

In a more specific context, the questions might sound something like "We're doing formative assessment"—yes, but how will your investment in the technology of assessment influence teachers' knowledge and skill, the level of content you expect to see in the classroom, and the role of the student in the instructional process? "We're focusing on developing strong instructional leaders"—yes, but what actual practice that will lead to improvements in content, knowledge and skill, and student engagement are you asking leaders to engage in? "We're adopting a new, more challenging math curriculum"—yes, but how would you know whether the instructional practice on which the curriculum is predicated is actually occurring in classrooms, and with what level of depth and consistency?

THIRD PRINCIPLE: *If you can't see it in the core, it's not there.*

The third principle is, in general, a good rule for the design of large-scale improvement strategies. It doesn't matter how much money you've spent. Nor does it even really matter whether everyone thinks it's a fantastic idea (since many people like best the changes that are the least disruptive). And, above all, it doesn't matter whether everyone else is doing it. What matters is whether you can see it in the core. If you can't, it's not there.

The instructional core also helps us predict what we would expect to see happening to student learning over time. Here the central idea is *the academic task*. As an example, one of our superintendents' networks was visiting a school in a network member's district. This particularly thoughtful and active host superintendent had managed to make quite a lot happen instructionally in his district in a relatively short period. In our visit, we broke into groups of three or four and did a series of rotations through classrooms, with two groups seeing each of four classrooms at a given grade level for a period of time. We then observed the team meeting of the teachers in the grade level whose classrooms we had observed. So, essentially, we saw the instruction in each classroom and then we saw the teachers talking about the instruction in their team meeting. Because the district and the school had worked hard on curriculum alignment, the teachers were able to talk about a common lesson sequence they were teaching and about the work that students were producing in that sequence, according to a common assessment that all the teachers were using. This is a rather sophisticated system.

In the team meeting, a problem emerged. The student work was obviously quite variable from classroom to classroom. In one classroom in particular, there were a number of students whose assessment results suggested that they apparently did not understand the content. The team leader asked the teachers what they thought explained the differences among classrooms. Each teacher offered an explanation. The explanations had mainly to do with the teachers' interpretations of the students' skill levels at the beginning of the unit. That is, the teachers felt that students who were struggling with the content had weak prior learning. So the discussion quickly shifted to what kind of remedial strategies one might use to bring those students up to the desired level.

What the teachers didn't know—because they had never observed each other teaching—was that the *actual work* that we observed students doing, within a nominally common curriculum framework, was quite different in each of the four classrooms. And the level of the student work that was presented at the grade-level meeting was quite close to the actual work that students were being asked to do in each classroom. In other words, the variability in student performance was a result of the teaching that was going on and the actual tasks that students were asked to do, *not*, as the teachers hypothesized, a result of the students' prior knowledge. This was yet more evidence for a simple, but powerful lesson—hold on to your hats—*teaching causes learning*. In the absence of direct evidence on what her colleagues were doing, the team leader, whose students produced the most consistently high-level work, was projecting her own practice onto the practice of the other teachers on the team. This led her to suggest that the variability couldn't be the result of differences in teaching, since "we're all teaching the same thing." In fact, they weren't.

What was different in the four classrooms was what exactly the students were being asked to do and the degree to which the teacher engaged students in the work by scaffolding their learning up to the complexity of the task. The curriculum was the same; the tasks were different.

In one classroom, the teacher took twenty minutes of the fifty-five-minute period explaining the task and directing students through a detailed procedural drill on what to do. The instructions were so complex that most students (and observers) couldn't repeat them when the children were released to work on their own. In another classroom, the teacher focused very little time on setting up the task, passed out the materials, and asked students to work individually on the task and to consult other students in their group if they got stuck. In yet another classroom, the teacher passed out the task, assigned roles to students at tables, and then circulated through the room answering individual students' questions.

In the team leader's classroom, the teacher spent less than five minutes reminding the students of how the task they were about to do was connected to the previous day's work, asked students what they had learned from that work, and then spent about five minutes walking students through a discussion of a model task that was similar to the one they were being asked to do. She then put students in groups, assigned roles, and circulated through the room. When we asked students in the first three classrooms what they were working on, none of them could reliably describe the task. When we asked students in the fourth classroom, they could reliably tell us what they were expected to do and tell us how it was connected to what they had done earlier.

It is important to add here that students in all four classrooms were "engaged," by conventional definitions—that is, they were attentive, nondisruptive, and compliant. If you were doing a windshield survey of classroom climate in this school, with the typical supervisory checklist, you would see, without exception, classrooms that were quiet and orderly and in which the teachers had done everything that the external environment expected of them. The "Do Now" was in the upper left-hand corner of the whiteboard; the specific objective of the day was prominently displayed, referenced to the appropriate state standard; the "Students Will Be Able to Do" was adjacent to the standard. If you stayed at the surface-level characteristics of the classroom, you would predict that students were all getting access to the same work.

But in reality, students were engaged in very different levels of work in different classrooms around a common curriculum unit. In the classroom where students were explicitly drawing on prior knowledge about how to address the task and where they had experience working individually and in groups, not surprisingly, they were relatively competent at doing what the teacher expected them to do, and they did it at a relatively high level. The teacher was free to work with individual students who were struggling with the task. Not surprisingly, things were different when the teacher was the main source of information on the task and the teacher's practice at setting up the task was disconnected from the students' understanding of it. Students were confused about the task and variable in their engagement with it. In our experience, the latter situation is much more common than the former in American schools. One of our favorite questions to ask students during an observation is "What's going on here?" The most frequent response is, "I don't know," or "Ask the teacher—she knows."

FOURTH PRINCIPLE: *The task predicts performance.*

doing the right thing & knowing the right thing to do.

What determines what students know and are able to do is not what the curriculum says they are supposed to do, or even what the teacher thinks he or she is asking students to do. What predicts performance is *what students are actually doing*. Memorization tasks produce fluency in memorization and recall, not necessarily understanding. Memorizing the elements of the periodic table is not the same as understanding the properties of the elements. The single biggest observational discipline we have to teach people in our networks is to look on top of the students' desks rather than at the teacher in front of the room. The only way to find out what students are actually doing is to observe what they are doing—not, unfortunately, to ask teachers what students have done after the fact or to look at the results of student work after they have engaged in the task. What was interesting about our observation with the superintendents' network was that for a brief moment, for this particular task, we, the observers, actually knew more about what was going on in these classrooms than the teachers did. This is an unsettling commentary on the instructional culture of American schooling.

Walter Doyle, from whom we have drawn most of our understanding of the nature of academic work, makes an interesting point about accountability:

Accountability drives the task system in the classroom. As a result, students are especially sensitive to cues that signal accountability or define how tasks are to be accomplished. In addition, students tend to take seriously only that work for which they are held accountable.[6]

What do our teacher hold their/our students/accountable for?

The accountability problem in the classroom is a microcosm of the accountability problem in the broader system. Other things being equal, people tend to want to do what they are expected to do in complex social systems with interlocking expectations. But to do what they are expected to do, they must know not only _what_ they are expected to do but also _how_ they are expected to do it, and what _knowledge and skill_ they need to learn how. This is the distinction that Nobel economist Thomas Schelling makes between doing the right thing and knowing the right thing to do. When we put teachers and students in situations where the task is vague and unspecified, but the expectations for performance are specific and high, we are expecting them to do the right thing without knowing the right thing to do. Students in three of the classrooms we observed that day were dutifully doing what they thought the teacher expected them to do, without knowing either what they were actually supposed to do or, more importantly *why* they should *want* to do it. We frequently see the same pattern with teachers—they are doing their best to do precisely what they think is expected of them without the *what* or the *why* being clear. This is a failure of the system, not of the teachers. Students in the fourth classroom had discussed how the task was related to the previous day's work and what they had learned from that work; they had seen and discussed a version of the task with the teacher *before* they were asked to work independently and in groups on the task. It was also clear from the way they worked that they were familiar with this routine. Notice also that the practice of the team leader did not trickle into the classrooms of the other teachers at her grade level—the culture of autonomous practice guaranteed that.

FIFTH PRINCIPLE: *The real accountability system is in the tasks that students are asked to do.*

This connection between doing the right thing and knowing the right thing to do leads to the fifth principle. From a policy and managerial perspective, we tend to think of accountability as a systemic issue. Accountability, in this view, is the way we steer the system toward a good collective result, using performance measures, standards, rewards, and sanctions. From this perspective, we tend to think that if we just get the incentives and structures right, good things will follow. In fact, this view of accountability rests on a heroic, largely unfounded assumption that students and teachers actually know what to do, that they know how to do it, and, most importantly, that they are able to derive some personal meaning and satisfaction from having done it. If you can't solve this problem of accountability at the classroom level, then the system-level work on accountability is mostly about the manipulation of political and managerial symbols, not about the improvement of learning.

In our experience working with teachers, principals, and system-level administrators around problems of large-scale improvement, people tend to be much more specific about what they expect by way of student performance than they are about what in classrooms would lead to the performance they desire. American schools have traditionally had an extraordinarily weak instructional culture, which has led, in turn, to extremely high variability in student performance among classrooms within schools, and to an extremely low capacity to affect instructional practice and student learning at scale. Trying to move performance in a system with a weak instructional culture is like pushing on a string. It doesn't do any good to know that there *is* an instructional core and that the tasks that students are asked to do within that core actually drive student learning, if the core itself differs from one classroom to another and if people aren't used to thinking about instruction as a collective practice.

This is why we have invested a good deal of our professional energy in building the competence of leaders in schools to observe, analyze, and affect instructional practice. We have deliberately drawn on the medical model in this work, not because we think educators ought to act more like physicians, but because medicine has, in our view, the most powerful social practice for analyzing and understanding its own work—the medical rounds model. In most instances, principals, lead teachers, and system-level administrators are trying to improve the performance of their schools without knowing what the actual practice would have to look like to get the results they want at the classroom and school level. We work with educators on the observation and analysis of teaching practice not because we think it's good for their souls (although it may be), but because we think you cannot change learning and performance at scale without creating a strong, visible, transparent common culture of instructional practice. And you can't create a common culture of practice without actually *engaging* in the practice yourself. We know this is heresy, since most administrators and support staff in schools choose to do what they are doing precisely because they see work in classrooms as too limiting. But this heresy leads to the sixth principle.

SIXTH PRINCIPLE: *We learn to do the work by doing the work,* **not** *by telling other people to do the work,* **not** *by having done the work at some time in the past, and* **not** *by hiring experts who can act as proxies for our knowledge about how to do the work.*

The genius of the medical rounds model is that the profession reproduces its practice and the surrounding culture through direct, face-to-face interactions around the work. To be sure, there is an ample supply of knowledge that comes from outside sources into the practice of physicians. And certainly, there are strong external controls and incentives that drive the practice in a given direction. But nested within these external structures and incentives is a social process for inducting people into the practice, for sustaining and developing norms of practice, and for making face-to-face evaluations of practice. The education sector, which is no less knowledge-intensive than medicine at its core, has no such culture-building practice. It should not surprise us, then, that the enterprise is atomized at its core. Education is essentially an occupation trying to be a profession without a professional practice.

When we work with people to develop their knowledge and practice around the instructional core, they typically ask two questions in the earliest stages of the work: "Can you tell us what high-level instruction looks like?" And, "How do I get people to do it?" People want an immediate framework for judging whether teachers are "doing it," and they want us to tell them how to get people who are not currently "doing it" to "do it." Our role is to disappoint people. We are fairly adamant in resisting answering these questions, to the point that it has become a standing joke in our practice. Why? Because we think people have to engage in sustained description and analysis of instructional practice before they can acquire either the expertise or the authority to judge it, much less to evaluate other people doing it. Most of the educators we work with—understandably, given the pressure they are under—want an immediate shortcut to the answer. You don't build a culture by taking shortcuts. It took over a hundred years to build the current dysfunctional instructional culture of American schools; it won't be transformed by taking a three-day or six-week course in supervision and evaluation.

SEVENTH PRINCIPLE: *Description before analysis, analysis before prediction, prediction before evaluation.*

You build a common culture of instruction by focusing on the language that people use to describe what they see and by essentially forcing people to develop a common language over time. Language *is* culture, and vice versa. When you jump straight from observation to evaluation, you short-circuit the difficult process of developing a common language to use in describing what you see going on in classrooms. In the absence of such a language, what you mean by some key term—*student engagement*, for example—might be completely different from what your colleague means by it, and you end up agreeing to disagree because it's too hard to figure out how to negotiate your differences. In our work, we insist that people develop a strong descriptive language and that they go through several iterations of a process for developing a common language *before* we move on to the tasks of analyzing, predicting, and evaluating (see chapter 4 for a deeper discussion of this process).

Analysis is getting people to work at grouping what they see into mutually agreed-upon categories and to start to make some judgments about how the categories are related to each other. *Prediction* is learning to use the evidence of observation and the analysis to make causal arguments about what kind of student learning we would expect to see as a consequence of the instruction we have observed. Typically, we ask people, "If you were a student in this classroom and you did exactly what the teacher expected you to do, what would you know how to do?" This question stems directly from the fourth principle—task predicts performance.

Only after people have developed the disciplines of description, analysis, and prediction do we raise the issue of evaluation, and then, we don't raise it in the typical form of "was this good teaching or not?" We ask people to address the question "What is the next level of work in this classroom, school, or system?" We pose the evaluative question in this way specifically to avoid the superficial classification of practice into "good," "mediocre," and "bad" because we want practitioners to think about the process of improvement as a *clinical practice*. That is, our job is to make the practice better over time, *not* to mete out rewards and punishments.

There is also an issue of humility involved here. Most of the people who, by virtue of their positional authority, are evaluating teachers could not themselves do what they are asking teachers to do. Teachers know this. The escalating demands of teaching practice are such that the knowledge and skill required to do the work is beyond both the experience and practical knowledge of the people charged with supervision. Creating a powerful culture of instructional practice in this situation requires supervisors to act as if they *don't* know; in this way, they learn what they need to know. Our most common advice to principals entering teacher grade-level meetings is, "Turn off your walkie-talkie, sit down, be quiet, and listen for at least ten minutes. Then, the first words out of your mouth should be a question to which you do not know the answer. "

Only after people have learned how to describe, analyze, and predict do we introduce specific frameworks for evaluating whether what we see is "high-," "medium-," or "low-level" practice.[7] Most people experience this process as unmooring, because most of their preconceptions about "high-level" practice can't actually be grounded in strong descriptive language. Having to make strong causal statements about what kind of teaching would produce a certain kind of learning usually results in considerable tightening and revision of people's initial conceptions of a strong practice. Another benefit of this discipline is that administrators who have to make decisions about who gets to tell teachers how to teach—consultants, coaches, curriculum developers, etc.—end up asking much tougher questions when they have been through the discipline of observation.

An example will illustrate. In our work with a principals' network, we spent about half of the first year of a two-year process focused on the descriptive/analytic phase of the practice. It was clear from the beginning that principals were intrigued by classroom structure and process. They thought that if you could just get a more predictable pattern of classroom process going, then you would get better results at scale.

So, not surprisingly, what jumped out of the initial observations was a lot of description of group work in classrooms, at the level of "students were sitting in groups doing their assigned work." When we pushed people to be more specific about what they saw and to predict what kind of student learning would result from this observation, they typically lost their traction. They couldn't say exactly what they would expect. So the next time, when they looked more closely at what students were actually doing in groups, the principals discovered (a now very robust finding in our work in schools) that the students were largely doing *individual* tasks while seated in groups. The nature of the task didn't seem to have anything to do with the students' being seated in groups, and the task itself seemed to be one that the students could easily do without much guidance from either the teacher or their peers. In other words, it didn't demand much in the way of cognitive engagement, either individual or collective.

With this discovery, the focus of the network shifted from the structure and organization of classrooms to the actual work that students were being asked to do, and the question shifted from "How is the classroom organized?" to "Does the organization of the classroom support the kind of work we expect students to do?" Instead of looking for a particular structure, the principals began looking for the task and hypothesizing about the structure that would go with the kind of task they were looking for. From then on, the work of the principals became much more focused on the actual work that students were doing and its relationship to what the administrators and teachers thought they were doing to support student learning.

So how does all this relate to the broader issue of organizing for large-scale improvement? The instruments that the typical state or local jurisdiction has available for school improvement are fairly blunt. You can tighten up on standards and incentives, raising the level of expected performance. You can clarify the content you expect to be covered at particular grade levels and adopt curriculum materials to support that. You can fill the system with information about student performance and create the expectation that people will use it to monitor and change their practice. You can provide training and professional development for teachers and administrators, and you can provide support for schools that are building higher-level instructional practice. You can release administrative control altogether on the theory that strong performance incentives will guide schools to the right result without guidance and support from the center. The aggregate effect of these measures is that some schools move in the desired direction; some essentially stay where they are in the distribution, which in the current accountability system means moving slightly forward; and typically, some schools actually continue to get worse against an increasingly challenging standard. This pattern describes what is currently happening in most large urban systems.

We do not think it is accurate to say that the improvement strategies in these systems have failed because they have produced this outcome. Rather, these improvement strategies have reached the limit of what they can produce with their existing theories of action. In most instances, when people ask us, "What more can we do at the system level to foster improvement in schools and classrooms?" our answer is, "Don't broaden the work with new initiatives; deepen the work with greater focus on building a strong culture of instructional practice." Most of the low-perform-ing schools in which we work don't need more programs or even, in most cases, more resources. In fact, part of the problem in these schools is that the presence of external support has actually increased the incoherence of an already incoher-ent instructional culture. These schools don't need more things to do. In fact, they need to do *less* with greater focus. They need a more powerful, coherent culture of instructional practice.

The pattern of improvement that we see in the aggregate with existing improve-ment strategies is a direct consequence of a chronically weak instructional culture. When you push hard on an essentially atomized culture with a strong set of exter-nal forces, you get a more atomized culture, not a more coherent one. The schools that are failing to respond to the best ideas about school improvement essentially have no capacity to mount a coherent response to external pressure, because they have no common instructional culture to start with. These are organizations for the private practice of teaching. The schools that are staying the same typically have figured out how to meet the requirements of the system without changing the default culture. They're able to stay in a zone where they don't have to challenge instructional practice, largely because they are producing performance with social capital, not instruction. And the schools that are getting better typically have man-aged to create, by their own devices, a more powerful instructional culture within their walls.

In no case has the improvement strategy directly addressed the issue of how to build a strong instructional culture at the system level that cuts across the boundar-ies of individual classrooms and schools. That is a much more complex task, requir-ing the creation of strong lateral relationships within and between schools designed around the development of a coherent instructional culture. In other words, it requires a *practice of improvement.*

In order for systemwide improvement strategies to work, they have to address the absence of a focus on the instructional core in the work of people in schools and in the work of people whose nominal job is to supervise and support schools. This means addressing the difficult task of building a common language of instructional practice, of building within and across schools the connective tissue by which the culture is propagated, of making the resources within the school and the system support the work of people around the development of practice, and of focusing greater attention on the knowledge and skill requirements of doing the work.

■

Tips and Takeaways

In summary, many forces in the name of "improvement" often pull the focus away from the instructional core. If this focus is lost, however, true instructional improvement is unlikely. Here are a few key points about the instructional core:

- *Focus on the core.* A focus on the instructional core grounds school improvement in the actual interactions between teachers, students, and content in the classroom, and provides a common focus in the practice of instructional rounds.

- *Task predicts performance.* The practice of instructional rounds provides a way of observing academic tasks, predicting what students will know as a consequence of what they are being asked to do, and providing guidance on the next level of work that would be required for students to perform at higher levels.

- *Accountability begins in the tasks that students are asked to do.* If the tasks do not reflect the expectations of the external accountability system, or our best ideas about what students should know and be able to do, then we should not expect to see the results reflected in external measures of performance.

We learn to do the work by doing the work, not by making more and more policies about the work, not by spending money on the next new idea about the work, not by asking people to do what they demonstrably do not know how to do and pretending that they do. What's more, we don't progress by claiming that things are getting better when one part of the distribution is improving and other parts are staying the same or getting worse. Instructional rounds is a practice that can be learned through repetition, reflection, and analysis at progressively higher levels of skill and knowledge. Rounds is a way of focusing on the instructional core of teachers and students in the presence of content.

CHAPTER 2

Theories of Action

There is nothing so practical as a good theory.
　　　　　—Kurt Lewin, *Field Theory in Social Science*

One year into her first superintendency, Helen Forsythe is confronting the difference between her vision for the Pleasanton schools and the facts on the ground. Her vision, stated in a compelling speech to the assembled teachers and administrators of Pleasanton at the beginning of her first year, was "to provide the highest-quality learning experience for every student, to make Pleasanton a beacon for successful teaching in literacy and mathematics, and to do so with respect for the judgment and competence of our professional staff. Together we can do this. Together we will." Behind these opening remarks was the reality that student performance in Pleasanton, as measured by the state competency exam, had been declining significantly in reading and math, and the proportion of high school students attending two- and four-year institutions after graduation had also declined. The district's demographics had also shifted, with the proportion of low-income students and English language learners increasing significantly.

When Helen surveyed the district's previous attempts to address instructional issues, she found a hodgepodge of special programs addressed to different target populations and considerable confusion at the school and classroom levels about how the district was handling its student performance problems. She quickly settled on a focused strategy of improved content and instruction in literacy and mathematics across the grade levels and announced it at the opening of school. Now, approaching the beginning of her second year, Helen noticed that principals and teachers didn't seem to understand the new focus. They referred repeatedly to the programs Helen had "shut down" and not to the new strategy. When Helen visited schools, she saw little evidence of the focus on literacy and math in classrooms. Her vision, compelling in principle, and her strategy, well worked-out conceptually, seemed not to have much reality on the ground.

Helen needs a theory. Her problem is one that most leaders confront. Their vision is, at least in their own minds, complete and compelling. The vision obviously worked in getting them into their jobs. But when the vision confronts the messiness of the actual organization, it seems less compelling. School systems and schools are not blank slates waiting to be written on by leaders. They are composites and collections of previous, often long-forgotten "solutions" to problems that other people thought were compelling at one time or another. The organizations embody beliefs and practices that are deeply rooted in people's identities and that can't be erased or displaced with a compelling alternative vision. Schools and school systems represent an equilibrium state—however dysfunctional—that accurately reflects the comfort zone of the people who work in them. Organizations resist "vision" not because of some perverse instinct on the part of people to resist change, but because the existing structures and practices provide a story line that people understand, and the vision often fails to provide an alternative that they find equally persuasive and understandable.

A theory of action can be thought of as the story line that makes a vision and a strategy concrete. It gives the leader a line of narrative that leads people through the daily complexity and distractions that compete with the main work of the instructional core. It provides the map that carries the vision through the organization. And it provides a way of testing the assumptions and suppositions of the vision against the unfolding realities of the work in an actual organization with actual people.

The term *theory of action* comes from the work of Chris Argyris and Donald Schön in their studies of individual and organizational learning.[1] They distinguish between individuals' theories of action, which describe people's implicit or explicit models of how they *intend* to act in the world, and their "theories in use," which describe how people *actually* act. Argyris and Schön focused largely on the learning processes by which individuals close the gap between their theories of action and theories in use. In describing this process of learning, Argyris and Schön distinguish between single-loop and double-loop learning. Single-loop learning describes the situation in which we act on the world, receive feedback on the consequences of our actions, and adapt our behavior to the feedback. Double-loop learning is the process of single-loop learning with the additional stage of *reflection* on the *process* by which we read and adapt to the consequences of our actions, and try to improve *how* we learn from our actions. These processes, Argyris and Schön argue, can be done at both the individual and the collective, or organizational, levels. The capacity to engage in double-loop learning, they argue, is what distinguishes more successful and less successful individuals and organizations. Hence, Argyris and Schön describe their approach to individual and organizational learning as "reflection in action."

In our work with instructional rounds, we focus a significant amount on getting participants to construct explicit theories of action and to assess these theories against the realities of their work. This work typically occurs after people have had some experience with the rounds process. As participants develop a facility with rounds, working in concert with their colleagues over several cycles of observation, description, analysis, and prescription, they develop some norms of collegiality and support. At this point, we ask them individually to develop their own theory of action about how their work relates *concretely* to the work of teachers and students in classrooms. We ask them to write down their theories of action in simple, descriptive terms. They then discuss those theories of action with their colleagues, typically in pairs and triads, and reshape the theories over time in response to their colleagues' feedback and their own experience. In this process, we hope to model the aligning of the *intended* theory the *enacted* theory through reflection in action.

In our framework, a theory of action has three main requirements:

1. It must begin with a *statement of a causal relationship* between what I do—in my role as superintendent, principal, teacher, coach, etc.—and what constitutes a good result in the classroom.
2. It must be *empirically falsifiable*; that is, I must be able to *disqualify* all or parts of the theory as a useful guide to action that is based on evidence of what occurs as a consequence of my actions.
3. It must be *open ended*; that is, it must prompt me to further revise and specify the causal relationships I initially identified as I learn more about the consequences of my actions.

We encourage people to state their theories of action as *if-then* propositions, in part to stress the causal nature of the statements and in part to reinforce that these are testable propositions that *should be* subject to revision if the goal is improved learning. The form seems a little stilted at first, but over time, people become more comfortable and fluent with it. They learn to develop and elaborate their if-then statements into more explanatory and challenging commitments and ideas.

A CAUSAL STORY LINE

Helen, the superintendent in the opening vignette, is not the only leader who needs a more explicit theory to make her vision and strategy more concrete. Take, for example, the case of a large urban district that decided it could affect the future educational attainment of its students by requiring that all students complete a rigorous algebra course before the end of ninth grade. Like Helen's vision, this was compelling, in large part because the district's data, and other evidence in general, suggested that whether and when students take algebra was a strong predictor of whether they would advance to postsecondary education. The vision was a long way from the facts on the ground. Many students in the system—perhaps as many as 40 percent—did not have the prerequisite math skills to take algebra. Part of the reason for the low achievement was a heavily tracked math curriculum before and during the middle grades that was a holdover from a previous era. Another reason was that the math instruction in the courses designed to prepare students for algebra was highly variable. There was support for the algebra-for-all vision among a significant minority of secondary math teachers, but most teachers still needed to be persuaded that the goal was feasible. The district needed a story line.

At a strategy session with system-level leaders, including the superintendent, the chief academic officer, and the people in the central office responsible for the algebra initiative, we asked what their theory of action was—how, exactly, would the system get from its current state to the one required by the vision? For example, how many new math sections would be required to accommodate the new students taking algebra? How many teachers would it take to staff these sections? How would the increases in algebra sections affect other math offerings? What would be the minimum amount of professional development required for teachers and principals to begin to adapt the existing algebra curriculum to a new clientele? How many coaches and professional developers would it take to meet those requirements? What would be the accountability expectations for schools around student enrollment and completion of algebra courses? What would constitute a quality experience for students taking algebra, and how would it be communicated and monitored by system-level and school-level leaders? How would the people responsible for the algebra initiative know whether the actual instruction met the requirements for a quality experience? What would happen when the inevitable breakdowns of logistics and organization occurred? Who would be responsible for fixing them?

As the questions rolled out, the assembled administrators looked stunned. Their implicit theory of action was something like "If the algebra-for-all vision is compelling and people have good motives and work hard, then students will take algebra and succeed at it." In our experience, this level of optimism about the direct relationship between a policy and student learning is common, and the people farthest from the daily interactions of the instructional core are most likely to unknowingly subscribe to the "and then a miracle happens" improvement theory. Many systems, like the algebra-for-all district, need a more explicit theory to make their good intentions a reality.

The more concrete the theory and the more it relates to the specific context in which participants work, the more likely it is to be useful. Often, participants start developing a theory of action at a fairly high level of abstraction: "If system and building level administrators monitor teaching practice in a serious and visible way, then teachers will teach high-level reading and writing skills, and then students will learn to write more fluently and powerfully." This might be a good start. First, it signals that the system is focused, at least for the time being, on reading and writing skills and it signals that teachers can't be expected to change the way they teach without challenge and support from administrators. But the theory doesn't deal explicitly with where teachers will get the new knowledge and skill necessary to do the kind of teaching required by the reading and writing initiative.

A give-and-take of the concrete details can deepen and refine the theory and make it more practicable. So colleagues might ask, "Where is the knowledge and skill to do this new kind of teaching going to come from?" To which the participant might respond, "If teachers have access to coaching and professional development focused on the core skills of high-level reading and writing, and if administrators monitor and support the acquisition of these skills through their daily visits to classrooms, then teachers will teach higher-level skills and students will demonstrate their learning by producing higher-level work." But, colleagues might ask, "Who gets to say what higher-level work might consist of, and how will we know it when we see it?". The participant might reply, "If teachers are knowledgeable about the performances that equate to high-level reading and writing and if they participate in the development of assessments that provide evidence of those performances, then they will know how to test their own knowledge and skill against the requirements of the new curriculum." And so on.

It is important for individuals to commit to a theory of action in written form, if for no other reason than it is easy to speak in causal terms when you're not actually required to write anything down. The act of writing itself forces individuals to confront the gaps and holes in their espoused theories and to think hard about exactly what they might mean when they say something like, "I regularly monitor the progress of principals in their school improvement plans." What exactly does it mean to monitor progress on a plan? Where does this occur? Does it occur in the principal's office after a series of classroom visits, or does it occur in the superintendent's office, with the principal reporting on what is happening at the school? What happens as a consequence of this monitoring? What evidence is there that monitoring influences principals' practice and that changes in principals' practice influence changes in teachers' instructional practices and student learning? How would we know when a particular approach to monitoring improvement plans was working? What are *you* and the principal actually learning in this process? What would we take as evidence of this?

The point here is not to develop a definitive theory that is useful once and for all time. It is, rather, to put into words the steps and contingencies that have to be mastered in order for a broad vision or strategy to result in concrete action that influences student learning. It is more important to have tried to figure out these contingencies than it is to find exactly the right expression for them. Theories of action should be, and will be, revised in light of experience.

One of the activities our rounds participants do is make an inventory of all the districtwide initiatives they are currently engaged in. The participants write down these initiatives on sticky notes, which are then put on a sheet of flip-chart paper and arrayed in relation to the participants' theory of action, which was developed earlier. What quickly becomes evident in such exercises is that the number of distinct initiatives is, for the typical district or school, significantly more that any single person can keep track of at one time. This is no real surprise—most organizations don't grow by design; they grow through opportunistic responses to their environments. And in most school systems, initiatives sprout like kudzu. Most projects have a deep history in the organization—a great idea that seemed to make sense at the time, a funding opportunity too good to pass up, a special project of a particular board member who used it as a way of getting elected, a state or federal mandate that has to be shoehorned into the organization chart, a particularly powerful and well-connected internal constituency that has managed to stake out a position in the organization chart, or the occasional project that time forgot. The job of a good theory of action is to find a clear path through this initiative thicket.

The essential principle of a theory of action is that it provides a *through-line* to the instructional core—what are the vital activities that need to happen to improve teaching and learning? A good theory of action connects an important part of the overall strategy to the actions and relationships critical to good performance. When they try to array initiatives against their theory of action, people usually have a very difficult time figuring out where some of those initiatives belong, including some number of "orphans" that don't actually fit very well. In fact, the better the theory of action, the more orphans it is likely to produce. That is, much of the clutter of programs, projects, and initiatives that constitute the typical organization chart of a school or system doesn't lie on the through-line that connects the organization's vision and strategy to the instructional core. How to clean up the organizational clutter that is exposed through a good theory of action is beyond the scope of this book, but in our networks, the developing of theories of action has had an impact on how participants have redesigned their organizations.

A corollary of the through-line principle is that it is *not* the job of a good theory of action to make sense of the clutter in an organization. There is often a temptation in the early stages of creating a theory of action to make a list of all the treasured and protected initiatives in a school or a system and then try to shoehorn them into a theory of action. This is the strategic equivalent of cleaning up your garage or your basement storage room—it is a laudable and virtuous activity, it makes you feel good when it's over, but it won't necessarily help you find a clear path to the instructional core. Whatever the specific problems of clutter in a given organization, instructional improvement requires a clear through-line to the instructional core, even if that involves pushing some treasured initiatives or orphans aside for the moment.

Another corollary of the through-line principle is that good theories of action tend to tighten up accountability relationships in the organization because the theories show how people in different roles must depend on one another to get a good result. In one district, the leadership team initially thought that by providing a high-quality curriculum and introducing the expectation that teachers would participate in professional development, the team would see good results in the classroom. What it discovered through rounds visits was that there were several breakdowns in that model—principals and teachers were not on the same page about the quality of the professional development, expectations about what role the principals would play in the roll-out of the curriculum were unclear, and the district's relationship with the professional development vendor was too loose. Once these contingencies were clear, it was possible to come up with some ideas about how to make key accountability relationships work and, more importantly, what support principals and teachers needed in order to be accountable.

Theories of action can also serve as glue for accountability relationships, particularly when the theories are made public. It is not unusual for superintendents we have worked with to make their theories of action available to people who work in the system. Theories by nature are unfinished products, hypotheses that may be wrong—sharing them is a form of making practice public that many people initially find scary. The more explicit that people are about their theory, the easier it is for others to hold them accountable for getting the desired result—and for following the through-line. Nevertheless, once rounds participants get over their initial hesitation, theories of action enter the language and the bloodstream of the organization. Participants often begin to develop theories of action with people in their systems. It is not unusual now to walk into a school in one of these systems, and to have the principal of that school present you with his or her theory of action.

Table 2.1 and figure 2.1 illustrate how this relationship between district- and school-level theories of action has played out in one Connecticut district—Farmington—where the superintendent, Robert Villanova, and the deputy superintendent, Eileen Howley, have worked over several years to bring system-level and school-level administrators into a working relationship around instructional improvement. The school-level theory of action is the result of Peter Cummings, the principal of West Woods Upper Elementary School, who is a relatively new principal, but a longer-term leader in the district. The Farmington leadership team, composed of key central office staff, principals, and assistant principals, does school visits and instructional rounds as part of its regular meetings. These meetings reinforce the common themes of the district's strategy and theory of action and provide principals with the opportunity to develop their theories of action tailored to the specifics of their school.

Looking at table 2.1 and figure 2.1 can be more than a little daunting if you've never developed a theory of action. It's important to understand that the Farmington

TABLE 2.1   TWO THEORIES OF ACTION

District-Based Theory of Action

1. If I/we create environments of shared collaboration focused on improving standards, curriculum, instruction, and assessment, then shared responsibility and shared accountability will create urgency for change and support continuous improvement of learning for all students.

2. If I/we cultivate expertise in teaching and learning as the means for improving student achievement, then teaching will be strengthened and more students will learn in deeper ways that better approach the "essential understanding" of the standards.

3. If I/we use data in systemic ways as a vehicle for examining school, classroom, and individual student progess, then interventions will be targeted in focused ways and achievement will increase.

4. If I/we foster a belief system driven by the principles of efficacy, hard work, and persistence, then we will increase student efforts to apply themselves to the work in focused ways and promote their achievement and mitigate against low expectations for student achievement.

School-Based Theory of Action

1. If we devote resources and time to developing the capacity of our teacher leaders to facilitate ongoing instructional improvement, then the focus of our teachers' regular work together will be grounded in improving learning experiences for all students.

2. If we continually develop the instructional expertise of our teachers, then teaching will be strengthened and all students will learn in deeper and more meaningful ways.

3. If we monitor students' progress through multiple formats over time, then we will be able to assess our instructional effectiveness and develop focused intervention strategies.

4. If we develop the efficacy of students so that they become active participants in their learning, then students will fully engage in school and develop the habits of mind that lead to successful lifelong learning.

5. If we develop a school climate and culture where every student and his or her family feel a sense of belonging, then families will join as partners in meeting the academic and social needs of early adolescents.

Adapted with permission from Peter J. Cummings, Principal, Farmington, Connecticut, School District.

FIGURE 2.1   DETAILS OF POINT 2 OF THE SCHOOL-BASED THEORY OF ACTION

2. If we continually develop the instructional expertise of our teachers, then teaching will be strengthened and all students will learn in deeper and more meaningful ways.

- We will embed ongoing professional development in our regular schedule (content area meetings, team meetings, faculty meetings) and specifically develop teachers' pedagogical content knowledge in reading, writing, math, science, and social studies.
  - □ Sixth grade content area meetings in writing and math
  - □ Faculty meetings devoted to instructional practice
- We will work with resource teachers to develop and implement specific content models of good instruction tailored to the upper elementary level.
  - □ Developing concepts of Teaching For Understanding through collaborative coaching and implementation of new curricula
  - □ Creating and coordinating professional development so that there is a common focus on the "big ideas" of upper elementary instruction, while exploring how instruction should be tailored to content in each area
- We will work with team leaders to develop their group facilitation skills and implementation of a collaborative planning model.

Adapted with permission from Peter J. Cummings, Principal, Farmington, Connecticut, School District.

---

theories come from a system that has worked long and hard on its improvement strategy with stable leadership and deep professional development, coupled with thoughtful recruitment and development of school leadership. The resulting theories are a result of an iterative process. Most initial attempts at developing theories of action don't look like this. They look more like the earlier examples of simple if-then statements that attempt to capture the crucial relationships if the intentions embedded in vision statements and strategies are to reach the instructional core.

THEORY OF ACTION AS A FALSIFIABLE HYPOTHESIS

When working with practitioners on their individual and collective theories of action, one quickly discovers that grand strategies of improvement at the system and school level typically lack enough operational detail to help people understand what the story line behind the strategy is and whether the strategy is working. In delving into the second key component of a theory of action, that it be falsifiable, one should distinguish between the vision that informs the strategy, the strategy itself, and the theories of action that operationalize the strategy. The vision might be at a very high level of abstraction: "Our students will develop the knowledge and skills required to be self-sufficient, responsible, and competent citizens in the twenty-first century." The strategy states the broad outlines of how the vision will be achieved: "Our focus for the next five years is raising the level of content and pedagogy in core academic subjects and measured performance for all students to world-class standards through investments in teachers' knowledge and skill and through the development of leadership capacity at all levels of the system." Buried in this strategy are a host of contingencies, like those outlined above in the algebra-for-all example, that someone will need to address in order for the strategy to work.

Theories of action might emerge while you are trying to make the strategy work in specific settings. So, for example, one problem that routinely arises when systems undertake ambitious improvement efforts is that the systems' capacity to deliver on the knowledge and skill required to improve instruction at the classroom level falls short of what is needed to make the strategy work. Sometimes, this shortfall is the result of an underestimate of how complex the actual work of teaching is. Sometimes, predictable logistical snafus limit professional development, and sometimes the relationships between the parties who have to work together to bring about the desired results falter. Teachers and administrators might see these problems become manifest in student performance, in the participation or lack thereof of teachers and principals in professional development, or in classroom practice that doesn't represent what they were hoping for. Observations of classrooms and of teacher and administrator team meetings might show that while the language that teachers and administrators are using to describe what they are doing corresponds to the lofty goals of the vision and the strategy, the actual practice in the classroom doesn't. Again, this is not an unusual occurrence in our experience.

The rounds process, then, might result in a revision of the superintendent's theory of action to place more emphasis on monitoring the quality of professional development and the level of support that teachers and principals receive in understanding and implementing higher-level instruction in the classroom. "If professional development occurs close to the setting in which the knowledge and skill will be used, and if teachers and administrators have regular and frequent observation and support from knowledgeable coaches, then instruction will begin to reflect the knowledge and skill we expect students to master." This theory of action is, notably, tailored to solving a central issue that arises in the enactment of the strategy. It allows the superintendent, the principals, and the teachers to focus on a specific line of causality that might connect what the system is doing with what the school is doing with what is going on inside the classroom. Furthermore, the theory of action is falsifiable in the sense that we can monitor whether moving the professional development closer to the classroom really does make a difference and whether a higher frequency of interaction between teachers and administrators around instructional practice has greater impact on student learning. If it doesn't, then we need to move to the next level of detail, or back off and try another theory.

Here's an example from our own practice. Early in our work with the Cambridge Leadership Network—which is composed of principals and central office staff, including the superintendent—the problems of practice that principals were coming up with prior to our rounds visits began to clump up around issues of math instruction. The district, under the leadership of its superintendent, Tom Fowler-Finn, had undertaken an ambitious strategy to improve teaching and learning in literacy and math. The strategy involved extensive investments in teacher professional development and the adoption of very ambitious, high-end curricula. During our rounds visits, we noticed that literacy instruction was developing more or less according to plan, but that math instruction was not. Math instruction was highly variable from classroom to classroom and, at its best, did not represent what the designers of the curriculum expected. During one of our debriefing sessions with the network participants, the principals raised this issue and an interesting discussion ensued.

"How many principals had done the professional development for the literacy strategy?" we asked. All the hands went up. "How many principals had done the professional development for the math strategy?" Two of twelve hands went up. "What were the participation rates of teachers in the professional development?" It turned out that many teachers were not showing up for the professional development sessions they were signed up for, pleading that they could not be out of their classrooms on the designated days.

As the debriefing discussion developed, several things became evident. The principals were uneasy about their own knowledge of math instruction. Teachers were uneasy about the new curriculum and its expectations for their own knowledge of math. Parents were starting to complain about the lack of focus on computational skills in the new curriculum. The teachers were avoiding the professional development, in part because the word was out that the quality of the professional development was variable. The professional development and coaching in the literacy strategy was considered exemplary by teachers, and the math work suffered by comparison. At some point in the debriefing, it became clear that the theory of action that had informed the literacy work wasn't working for math—different context, different set of problems, different set of base conditions of teachers' knowledge and skills. At that point, the superintendent and principals began to craft a new approach to implementing the math strategy. The principals resolved to spend the next year working on their own math knowledge. The central office staff renegotiated their relationship with the math professional development provider to include tighter quality control and more responsiveness to the district's agenda. The principals began to listen more carefully to the teachers' views on the curriculum and the quality of the professional development. And after several more rounds visits, the network developed much more explicit language about what it was looking for as evidence of high-level math instruction and student learning.

What was happening here was the network was tuning its theory of action, which was derived in part from the literacy work, to a new situation. The initial theory of action might have been something like: "If we adopt a well-designed reading and writing curriculum, and provide high levels of professional development and support for teachers in learning how to use it, then we will see changes in instruction consistent with our aspirations for student learning and increases in higher-level reading and writing skills for students." The tuned theory of action had to allow for the possibility that the problems of accountability and knowledge were more formidable in the math strategy than in the literacy strategy: "If we adopt a well-designed math curriculum, and if we understand the knowledge and skill gaps that have to be filled in order for teachers and principals to master the curriculum, and if we provide and carefully monitor the quality of the professional development, and if we develop clear accountability expectations around participation in professional development, then we will see changes in instructional practice consistent with our aspirations for student learning and increases in higher-level math skills for students." Over the next year, the Cambridge network crafted all its problems of practice around math instruction, principals and central office staff worked out detailed descriptions of what they expected to see in classrooms as evidence of high-level math instruction, and the district's curriculum specialist helped develop several sessions around mathematics content and pedagogy.

The Cambridge example illustrates how a powerful vision and a well-worked-out strategy in one domain may not work equally well in another domain. It also illustrates how the rounds process can be used to tune a strategy to the particular circumstances of a new line of work. And it illustrates how rounds can create a culture of collaborative problem-solving when discussions are about the actual instruction in classrooms as opposed to people's projections of their own ideas about what's happening in classrooms. But the main lesson from the Cambridge example is that the drive for specificity and discipline that comes from a close examination of whether a theory of action is working (in other words, testing the hypothesis) carries rewards in increasing the connection of vision and strategy to practice.

In our rounds, we try to model the development of theories of action as a process of serial learning over time. We ask people to make a simple initial statement of their theory and to share it with one or two of their colleagues, using a protocol of presenting and then listening to colleagues talk about what they see in the theory—much the same as we try to stay primarily in the descriptive voice when we speak about instructional practice on our rounds visits. We do not have hard-and-fast rules about whether participants should make their theories of action public, but most participants do at one stage or another of development. As noted above, in the Connecticut Network, all participants use their theories of action with their senior leadership teams, and many participants have led principals in their districts through the process of developing their own.

In the Cambridge example, the discovery that a relatively simple theory that seemed to work for literacy does not work for math underscores the importance of falsifiability. We should be able to discover, as we have now in many observations, that putting teachers in teams to do grade-level or content-level common planning, does not, other things being equal, make instruction more coherent across classrooms. We should be able to discover that providing off-site professional development in a key instructional domain—no matter how good—does not provide teachers and principals with answers to the critical issues of practice they face when they try to put the ideas into play in classrooms. Notice, it is *not* that the initial theories are necessarily *wrong*. In fact, there are compelling reasons for districts to continue to invest in high-quality, professional development and to put teachers in teams for common planning. The problem is that the theories of action that informed the use of professional development and common planning time were underdeveloped. We can only learn that they are underdeveloped and what to do about it by initially stating what we think we are doing and then testing our theories against the reality of the environment in which they have to work. The principle of falsifiability allows us to take our best ideas into practice, to see where they break down, and to modify them in light of experience.

REVISING THE THEORY OF ACTION AND DOUBLE-LOOP LEARNING

While having a falsifiable, if-then causal statement is a good start, it is the act of repeatedly revisiting the theory in the presence of colleagues that matters most for people's learning. In the process of successive revisits, the actual written version becomes an artifact or a proxy for a more complex cognitive and emotional learning process—a kind of life ring available to the practitioner when the water gets rough and evidence of success is scarce. People learn to treat their theories of action as touchstones for their own professional and cognitive development, as works-in-progress along a path that leads through successively greater levels of understanding of the work. In this sense, if you tend to your theory of action over time, it becomes like a diary, a record of the progression of learning in practice.

The requirements of open-endedness and successive discussion and revision are important for two reasons: First, these norms model the process of double-loop learning. If practitioners see their theory of action as a "finished product," suitable for framing and public display, then it ceases to function as a learning tool and it becomes a symbolic artifact, useful primarily as a tool for legitimizing their authority. "This is my theory, and I'm sticking with it." The norm of open-endedness suggests that developing your practice is a continuous process over time and that, no matter how successful you think you are, there is some set of problems you have not yet come to terms with. Second, open-endedness and successive discussion and revision are important because they model knowledge and skill in practice as a *collective*, rather than an individual good. That is, if you return to your colleagues on a regular basis for consultation, it creates the expectation that you will have something to say about your learning. It also creates the expectation that your colleagues are engaged in a process of learning, and if *you* show up with something interesting to say about your learning, *they* should also have something to say about their learning. Over time, people learn that it is acceptable to incorporate other peoples' ideas into their own practice and to ask advice from their colleagues about particularly intractable problems they are facing.

The purpose of developing and using theories of action, according to Argyris and Schön, is not just to test our theories against the reality of the environment, but also to build our capacity to reflect on the process of learning itself and to begin to build an understanding of how each of us develops his or her practice. If the conversation and action were to stay at the level of successive problem solving, then we would have what Argyris and Schön call a robust practice of single-loop learning. That is, each successive problem-solving episode would constitute a single, isolated improvement event, not necessarily connected to the others. Cumulative learning, they argue, occurs when the events are connected, individually and collectively, by reflection not only on the solutions to specific problems but also on improving the learning that enables solutions to emerge. With practice and successive iterations, participants begin to reflect not only on the causal connections between what they do and what happens in classrooms, but also on how the participants learn to adapt their practice to the challenges being surfaced. Good theories of action, then, become distillations of the individual and organizational learning that comes with rounds.

Double-loop learning must be iterative. Doing something "right" the first time doesn't necessarily mean that powerful learning is occurring. It might mean that we didn't risk enough in stretching our own capacity to handle unfamiliar situations. Real learning occurs through a process of trial and error, working at or close to the boundaries of our own knowledge and competence, and paying attention to the evidence of whether our predictions about what will happen next are accurate. The world of school culture, unfortunately, does not reward or reinforce this kind of risk-taking behavior. Making mistakes is, more often than not, interpreted as a sign of incompetence, not of learning. It would be useful if the culture of schools were more forgiving around learning, but in the short term, we can't wait for the culture to transform itself in order to get on with instructional improvement.

Instructional rounds can be a safe haven for double-loop learning in a culture that is generally hostile to it. We try in our work to create an atmosphere in which participants can share their best ideas about their practices and discuss their most problematical and difficult failures and face-plants. We stress norms of confidentiality: No discussion of specific individuals or specific problems outside the network unless by explicit permission of the person involved. In discussion and analysis, we use protocols that allow individuals to participate within a well-defined and safe structure. And over time, we have discovered that people learn how to present their most difficult and problematical issues to their colleagues and to give and receive feedback in a critical but not hostile environment. In the Connecticut Superintendents' Network, we keep verbatim transcripts of our discussions and debriefings, and we routinely discuss excerpts from our prior discussions, critiquing our work according to the norms we have agreed upon.

As the work of instructional rounds becomes more focused on the actual improvement of instruction, and as participants begin to see the results of the work for their own practice, the immediate demands of single-loop learning (i.e., connecting the dots from the vision to the strategy to the practice) tend to displace the more abstract demands of double-loop learning—the opportunity to reflect candidly about what we are learning about our own learning. Hence, it is important to routinely save space in the agenda of rounds meetings for reflections on practice, process, and learning and to create strong norms of candor and confidentiality to support those discussions.

In our practice, we begin at the individual level of constructing a theory of action, because if individual leaders can't clearly describe what they are trying to accomplish, it is highly unlikely that the organizations they lead will behave coherently. But it is also evident that as the practice of individual leaders develops, the construction of a theory of action becomes a more collective effort in several senses. First, as we have seen, when superintendents develop and share their theories of action, principals often follow suit, either because they are interested in making their work visible, or because they are involved in networks in which it is an expectation. Second, as the Cambridge example illustrates, it often becomes necessary to pause in the course of some improvement effort that seems not to be working and consider the causal connections that are and are not occurring around the work. At this point, the leader's personal theory of action becomes, of necessity, the collective theory of action of the organization, and the various connections between one step in the process and another become, in effect, connections between one part of the system and another. Finally, the central issues of school improvement are cultural—that is, they involve getting people in the organization to examine the work of the organization with fresh eyes and to clear away much of the accumulated clutter from previous reforms to focus on the work of the moment. Theories of action can be important cultural artifacts in the sense that they make explicit the connections between the individual and organization—connections that are necessary to reach and improve the quality of instruction in the classroom.

■

Tips and Takeaways

A theory of action, then, is a set of causal connections, usually in the if-then form, that serves as a story line that connects broad visions with the more specific strategies used to improve the instructional core. The discipline of crafting a theory of action requires cutting through the predictable clutter of the organization to the set of actions critical to instruction and student learning. Good theories of action also tend to tighten up accountability relationships in the organization because they expose mutual dependencies that are required to get the complex work of instructional improvement done. Theories of action also provide the basis for single-loop and double-loop learning. They provide the opportunity to test our presuppositions about what we think will work against the evidence of what actually works. And they enable participants to reflect individually and collectively on their practice and the process of learning they are engaged in around their practice.

Here are a few key practical ideas to keep in mind as you try to develop theories of action in the context of instructional rounds:

- *A simple and incomplete theory is better than no theory at all.* It's hard to learn if you don't make mistakes, and it's hard to learn if you don't test your best ideas against reality. The process of developing a good theory of action is iterative for a reason—it is a learning process.

- *More heads are better than fewer.* Like the process of observing and analyzing instruction, the process of developing and testing a theory of action works better when it occurs in concert with other people who have different ideas, whose experiences can be used to inform your practice, and who might know some things that you don't know. Strong norms of confidentiality and candor make collegial discussions of theories of action more powerful.

- *Clutter is the enemy of clarity and coherence.* You may not be able to change the organizational clutter of the system all at once, but you can find a clear path through the clutter with a well-developed theory of action. The role of a theory of action is not to make sense of the clutter, but to cut through the clutter to the instructional core. Save the orphans for later, and don't let them get in the way of the strategy.

- *Share your theory of action inside and outside your organization.* Public discussions of your own learning model show other people the process you expect them to go through in the development of their own practice. Make your own theory public, and work with others to make theirs public, too.

PART 2

Doing Rounds

CHAPTER 3

Launching a Network

"Do you think anyone will sign up?" Deb worried for the thirteenth time. As the convener of rounds and a professor at the local university, she had a personal stake in the success of the model.

Her colleague Stella responded understandingly, "Come on, Deb. If we don't get many people who want to do rounds this first year, it's not necessarily a bad thing. Wouldn't you rather have a few fully invested people than a roomful of people who are going to come inconsistently and be checking their e-mail the whole day?"

Deb replied, "After the way you went over the rules at the information session last week, I don't think anyone would consider coming inconsistently! You made that one absolutely clear."

"I think that's part of what is tricky about launching this network," Stella said. "Some things we can mandate—attendance, hosting visits, the steps of the process, even. But the fundamental piece—whether people believe that this will help them learn and be worth their time—is ultimately up to each individual. I just hope we explained the process well enough so that people can make an informed decision."

Deb nodded. She and Stella had spent several days recruiting superintendents to the network, trying to convince them of the benefit of rounds. At the same time, she recognized the large time commitment involved. "I wish we could show them the network we saw last year. It was so exciting to see the superintendents talking about specific ways to support instruction. And the way they pushed each other—that was impressive, too."

"Well," said Stella, "we can't expect our group to achieve that level of candor and accountability to each other right away. I figure if we at least convinced people that

candor and accountability to a group of peers is a desirable goal and that rounds will help us get there, we're off to a good start. But we'd better get to that point pretty quickly, or people aren't going to want to stay around."

Bringing high-quality teaching and learning to scale in a district requires an enormous amount of new learning for everyone in the system. Coming from traditions of isolated and autonomous practice, many teachers and administrators are unfamiliar with visiting classrooms, talking about teaching and learning, devising systemic strategies for improvement, and refining theories of action over time. What is more, they are often unfamiliar with how to work well with each other in these endeavors and to learn from one another. We have found that networks of colleagues working together on common practice provide the best venue for this learning. To be effective at supporting and providing a context for the learning of instructional rounds, networks need to be connected to the instructional core, provide safe spaces for people to learn new approaches, and develop the kind of cohesion that lets participants support each other—and hold one another accountable—in their instructional improvement work.

How do you prepare for and launch such a network? Taking the time to prepare is essential, not just to ensure that you have a network *structure* that has the right people, clear guidelines, and access to the resources needed to support instructional improvement, but to make sure you are developing a network *culture* that allows participants to learn from and with each other. We emphasize culture because focusing on instructional improvement in a district requires an enormous amount of learning for everyone in the system. Creating an instructional rounds network is a lot more than gathering people to "do rounds." Most people in schools and districts work in siloed cultures characterized by independence and autonomy and don't always know how to work well with each other in their efforts at improvement. In many settings, it is difficult for educators to admit what they don't know, especially about improving instruction. Many administrators need to "unlearn" the judgmental observational practices that frequently characterize supervision. Sometimes, educators are not sure how to learn as a group in tackling new skills and acquiring new knowledge. Finally, without developing a different culture about it, rounds may be seen as another top-down "gotcha"—something that has happened with many forms of "walkthroughs." As you think about preparing and launching a rounds network, think about what it takes to build an organizational structure that can support the effort, as well as a different kind of culture. Think about how to create a network that moves away from the default mode of hierarchy, compliance, and self-protection and moves toward a culture that creates a safe space for individual and organizational learning.

This chapter answers many of the questions that arise when a group is forming instructional rounds networks, including these: How do you start? Who should be involved? How big should the network be? What kinds of resources, including time, are needed? In addition to these practical questions about size and structure, this chapter addresses the equally important issues of how you ensure that the group of people being assembled develops a culture that lets them learn about instruction and leadership practice from and with each other. For instance, what kinds of commitments and norms should the network have? How do you get buy-in from participants? What are the nonnegotiables for network development, and what can be adapted to meet local circumstances and needs? What needs to be established from the beginning, and what can the network define over time?

There is not one cookbook set of answers to these questions. Rather, this chapter draws on the experiences of four networks that are currently supporting instructional rounds—networks of differing sizes, membership composition, school-versus district-level focus, and stages of development—and shares the way they have answered these questions. While these four do not represent every possible configuration (e.g., we have not yet worked with a teacher-only network doing instructional rounds), readers should be able to see themselves in the different situations, learn from each example, and make choices that best meet their needs. The chapter also describes some of the key roles people will need to play, including the role of the network facilitator, and closes with some specific practical suggestions that our networks have found helpful for orienting people to the rounds practice and getting them ready to launch a network to support rounds.

Although each of the four networks we have worked with took a slightly different path to get organized, all of them faced a few core tasks necessary for any network start-up. Somebody or something—an individual or an organization—had to do several things:

- *Convene* the network, including recruiting a committed group of educators.
- *Muster and manage the resources*—time, space, facilitators, materials—to make the network viable.
- *Develop initial expectations and norms* around the deeper aspects of developing and supporting a network learning culture.

On the following pages, we provide examples of how each of the four networks approached these three broad network development tasks, along with our suggestions on the advantages and disadvantages of the choices, to help you make the best decisions for your situation.

CONVENING THE NETWORK

Somebody needs to convene the network. The organization may be an existing one that has added rounds to its activities, or might be specially created for the purpose of doing rounds. The four networks with which we have worked have each been convened with a slightly different variation: a district (Cambridge Leadership Network); a nonprofit that supports school improvement in many districts (the Connecticut Center for School Change); a set of existing regional organizations through which superintendents are affiliated according to geography (the Area Educational Agencies in Iowa); and a specially established rounds network supported by a state department of education (Ohio Leadership Collaborative). Each had or developed the convening authority and capacity to get people and resources necessary for rounds.

Networks must make decisions about membership, size, recruitment, and screening. Each of these is described in more detail below.

Membership

The first decision to make is who will be in the network, who won't be, and why. Your decisions have a great deal to do with who is convening the network, what its purpose and focus is, and if any particular membership is to be served. Networks might be role-alike, like the superintendents' networks in Connecticut and Iowa, or might be cross-role, as in Cambridge and Ohio. Role-alike networks have the advantages of, at least initially, greater comfort and safety. Superintendents, for example, are generally more likely to make themselves vulnerable with other superintendents without their direct reports or union leadership present. The same is true for principals or teachers, who are more likely to make themselves vulnerable if they are not with people with whom they have differential authority or an evaluative connection (either as evaluator or evaluatee). On the other hand, our experience suggests that when a cross-role network gels and gets over its initial discomfort, it can be a powerful tool for district-focused improvement; the diversity of roles that might create a more challenging start-up can be an asset in engaging others in the district and bringing about change in the long run.

Networks might be within a single system, like a district or school; across multiple systems; or in some combination of within-system networks that are linked to other networks (e.g., school-based networks connected within a district to other networks, or district-based networks connected within a state to other networks). Ohio started as a statewide network of district teams and embraced mixed teams, including teachers, union leadership, principals, superintendents and deputy superintendents. When it came time to plan its in-district networks, the Ohio group found its mixed-role membership helpful. Teachers and union representatives helped design and implement outreach to participating schools, and principals helped explain the model to their colleagues. Cambridge included central office personnel, the superintendent, union leadership, and principals, but chose not to include assistant principals, teachers, and some central office personnel, partly because of pragmatic size considerations and partly because the network wanted to focus on developing knowledge and skill in the instructional core with a particular group of leaders first. If our experience is any predictor, once the rounds practice roots, other educators will want in or will want their own network. It's useful to anticipate this and think about how you will respond to this rounds ripple effect from the time of initial launch. In Connecticut, when deputy superintendents became interested in participating in rounds, the Connecticut Superintendents' Network (CSN) decided to keep theirs a superintendent-only network, and a different deputy superintendent network was created. In Cambridge, assistant principals incorporated rounds visits into their existing monthly meetings. And in all of our networks, we've seen individual participants launch their own within-system networks with or without additional support—for example, superintendents launching principal or school-team networks, principals launching within-school teacher networks.

Size

Each circumstance is different, and you will need to figure out what works best in your situation. A key consideration is, How many school visits will the network do each year, and how long will it take to visit each participant's school/district? You want enough people to provide a range of experiences to learn from and not so many people that it takes too long for participants to host rounds visits. The balance of these is important for creating a rich environment of learning, support, and accountability. If it's four years between visits to a site, it's easier for hosts to see the network as an interesting learning experience as opposed to a place where they're focused on how their work affects the instructional core. Our networks have made different decisions, affected in part by who is in the network. The Cambridge network has about thirty members. While this sounds large, the school-based personnel (principals and high school deans of instruction) represent the district's fourteen schools, and the network visits each school once every two years. In Ohio, the initial network had five districts, each visited in the first year, and within-district networks are now being launched with varying sizes. Columbus, Ohio, for example, has launched two networks of about twenty-five people, with representatives from five schools each. In Iowa, the networks range from six to almost twenty. For many years, Connecticut had ten to twelve members, a cap that seemed necessary so that all the members could have their districts visited in a two- or three-year period. When the network decided to expand, it added a second cohort of twelve. The use of two parallel cohorts in Connecticut is one way to meet the likely demand to expand without losing the intimacy of a small network. Connecticut treats the groups both as one cohesive network that comes together four times a year for planning, reflection on network data, and common professional development and as two independent cohorts that do school visits and debriefs separately.

Basic Structure of the Network

One of the first questions potential members will ask is, How much time will it take? There is no set rule, but the short answer is that regular rounds practice takes a significant investment of time. Our networks commit at least a day a month, sometimes more, which is what it takes to engage in rounds visits and the professional learning and reflection that must accompany visits (table 3.1). Connecticut meets monthly from 8:30 a.m. to 1:30 p.m., alternating visit days with days for reflection, planning, and professional development. Each year, the two cohorts overlap for an opening session, a midyear (January) meeting, and a closing meeting, which along with a two-day annual retreat at Harvard, provide time for reflecting on the process and individual organizational learning, but make for relatively few school visits (four visits per cohort per year). Cambridge devotes full school days (8:00 a.m. to 3:00 p.m.) to monthly school visits, with time for professional learning and reflection built into that day, as well as half-day monthly meetings integrated with existing principal meetings. The statewide network in Ohio met twice for orientation and skill building, and then met monthly for five visits over the balance of the school year (one in each district). Each district decided how to structure its in-district rounds, framed by the overall expectation for five internal visits over the year. The Iowa format has been roughly similar, with two-day gatherings that include school visits and with different areas exercising local options for exactly how and when to structure their visits in the spin-off networks.

When you make your choices, think about geography (especially travel time—sometimes it's easier to have longer, less frequent days), how many schools or districts will be in your network, and how frequently each will be visited. Also factor in time for the nonvisit work—planning a visit, sharing content and just-in-time relevant professional development, reflecting on the learning of the network and its norms, and sharing reports about follow-ups to visits and the impacts of rounds on school and district practices.

Develop and Recruit Members

The second question potential members will likely ask is, Why should I do rounds? How will it help me help my students? You will need to help potential members develop a picture of what rounds is and is not, particularly when they have experience with something like walkthroughs that look like rounds but are quite different. We have found visiting existing rounds to be the best way for people to get a sense of what rounds offers. Follow this up with having people talk with others who have rounds experience (especially educators in similar roles to those in your prospective networks) and read about the rounds process. None of our networks has mandated rounds participation initially (though Cambridge now mandates participation for new hires). All the networks have included dialogue and an opting-in process. And all had early rounds champions, one or a few individuals who saw rounds as key for improving the instructional core and recruited others. In most of our networks, it took up to a year to develop the critical mass needed to form a network, get funding, and launch. Both Iowa and Ohio have used a staged scale-up model, where a set of participants engaged in rounds before recruiting others into spin-off networks. In Iowa, facilitators from all the Area Education Agencies (AEAs) sat in on, and participated in, the launch and the first two school visits of one AEA's network and used the exposure and knowledge they got to go back to recruit in their own areas. In many cases, the facilitators were joined at the cross-AEA launch by a superintendent from their own AEA, who could describe the practice to his or her colleagues back home. In Ohio, as districts launched their own within-district networks, some districts developed an outreach strategy to inform the entire district about rounds,

TABLE 3.1   SAMPLE DECISIONS FROM FOUR NETWORKS

Network Site	Who Participates?	Frequency and Format of Meetings?	Who Facilitates?	Content Focus?
Connecticut	Superintendents (2 cohorts of approx. 12 superintendents each)	Monthly Alternate site visits with debrief sessions	Harvard team	Varies; recent focus on teams
Cambridge, MA	All principals, super-intendent, deputy superintendent, district curriculum directors, union president (about 30 participants)	Monthly full-day site visits and debrief Monthly half-day professional development session	First two years: Harvard team Subsequently: the deputy superinten-dent and a retired principal	Math
Ohio	Year 1: Cross-role teams from 5 districts with 5 members on each team including at a minimum: super-intendent, principal, teachers union repre-sentative Year 2: Cross-role teams from 4 districts with 9 members on each team	Year 1: Approxi-mately monthly full-day meetings with site visit and debrief Year 2: Quarterly meetings of 2 days each with site visit and debrief on day 1, profes-sional development and leadership development on day 2; within-district rounds meet for five or more additional visits and debriefs	Year 1: Harvard team Year 2: Harvard team; simultaneous in-district networks facilitated by local staff developers hired by districts	Informally during year 1: higher-order thinking Formally year 2: twenty-first-century skills
Iowa	Superintendents (cohorts of approx. 16)	Varies by Area Educational Agency	First four sessions: Harvard team Subsequently: regional directors and regional profes-sional developers	Varies by Area Educational Agency

even though not all schools would be involved in rounds initially (see, for example, exhibit A.1 in the appendix).

Decide on a Screening Mechanism and/or Clear Commitment to Participation

It is important for any network to have a committed, stable set of members. A key consideration is whether the network is open to everyone in your target audience and whether there is any sort of entrance requirement. In our experience, it helps to have some sort of entry threshold of readiness or commitment that is demonstrated prior to admission.

The demonstration of commitment can take several forms. In Cambridge, the principals looked at a few models of observing and discussing teaching and together decided to commit to instructional rounds. In Ohio, the state department of education invited the "Ohio Eight," the largest urban districts in the state, along with one smaller district that had preexisting connections with many of them, to apply for the network. In their application, the districts outlined their improvement strategy, committed the time of their five-person team (including the superintendent) to all rounds sessions, and agreed to host a visit, start an in-district rounds program in the second year, and pay a portion of the costs. The Iowa AEAs make clear that all superintendents are welcome if they agree to a set of expectations, have the required board president endorsement, and have some type of plan for instructional improvement (see exhibit A.2, the application for the Iowa Leadership Academy, in the appendix). The Connecticut Center for School Change invites its members selectively. It annually requests nominations from its members to fill any openings, and then screens candidates with a site visit and an opportunity to make the expectations and norms clear. Superintendents are expected to have, or to develop, a theory of action for instructional improvement as a ticket of entry.

Figuring out how you want to address the above convening tasks represents your critical first steps in launching your rounds network. These are important decisions, and your individual circumstances will shape not just what you decide, but how you decide. The approach you use for making these decisions for a single district will be different than if you are launching a dozen regional networks for superintendents within the same state, where you will need to agree, as they have done in Iowa, on what decisions will be made collaboratively (and will be applied to all networks) and which will be locally determined. While the convening steps outlined above will help you launch your network, there are a number of other considerations to make sure that your network has the structural and cultural elements to support the rounds process and maximize the impact it can have on improving the instructional core in your setting. These are explored in the next two sections.

MUSTERING AND MANAGING RESOURCES

Schools and districts are places where resources are in short supply, and there is no shortage of demands on them. To provide sufficient structure to support rounds, networks need access to a number of important tangible resources: time, money, materials, space, and facilitation. To increase the chances that rounds actually improve school and district performance, networks also need a less tangible but even scarcer resource in many settings—focused and prioritized attention. As you figure out how to muster and manage the resources needed to support a rounds network, keep in mind the challenge of developing and keeping focused attention on rounds as a central part of school and district work.

Participant Time

The biggest resource cost, and usually the hardest one for participants to commit to, is the time of the participants themselves. Medical rounds are part of being a medical professional, and doctors don't miss rounds, but that is not how most educators see rounds, at least initially. For an in-district network like Cambridge, having central office staff and principals participate for a day and a half a month is an enormous commitment of time and money and speaks to the value that both the superintendent and participants place on rounds. Getting high-level commitment to rounds is important in helping individuals see that their involvement with rounds is considered their core work and not some marginalized add-on. It is not always easy. One superintendent has told us that his school board is so against anything that sounds like professional development for him that he almost has to sneak out to rounds network meetings. A central office administrator who has been a tireless and passionate advocate and worker for rounds tells us that her boss does not value it and never asks about the rounds work at staff meetings. "I bring it up anyway," she says, "because it is an important part of where the district is going— but I know my boss doesn't like it when I do." Superintendents, especially for in-district networks, can send clear messages to their own staffs about the importance of rounds—as one of the superintendents in Ohio did by listing rounds as one of the three most important district priorities.

There is also some balancing that has to go on: How much time should participants commit to rounds, given the other demands on their time? As the in-district networks in Ohio get launched, one of the biggest concerns expressed by the teachers who are being asked to join rounds is the number of days out of their classrooms. Network planners have made trade-offs between the maximum—how many days over the year they can ask teachers to be out of classrooms—and the minimum number of visits they feel are needed to get traction and momentum going. (They came up with five visits per year.) You and your network will need to manage the cost-benefit equation inherent in a time-consuming instructional improvement approach like rounds, especially in the beginning, when participants are not yet clear on the benefits they may get from doing it. You may be able to think creatively about time and integrating rounds into existing work by repurposing existing meeting times to rounds.

Money, Materials, and Space

Networks need access to space, staff support, supplies, food, and all the other necessities of bringing people to work together periodically for a day or more. Participants have used a variety of models to organize meetings. In Connecticut and Iowa, existing infrastructures are used (the Connecticut Center for School Change, the Area Educational Agencies); Cambridge uses its district structure and resources; and Ohio uses the Ohio Department of Education as the fiscal agent, with food and materials expenses associated with each visit absorbed by the hosts.

Networks also need the ability to collect and expend funds for outside facilitation, travel, materials, and other meeting costs (that are not supported by participating districts); staff support time that is not being offered as in-kind; any documentation or evaluation efforts, and so on. As you think about meeting these cost challenges in your network, use the design elements you identified as important as you read this chapter to help you draft a budget. How often will you meet? Will travel be involved? Will you be using internal or external facilitators, and how much will you need to pay them? Where will food, chart paper, and other supplies like technology come from? Overall, how much of the costs will be borne by the network and by its members? How much can you use existing structures and personnel to support the network, and how much will you need to create anew? What are the costs to launch versus to maintain the network?

Facilitation

Next to participants' time, the most expensive resource in a network is facilitation. Instructional rounds requires skilled facilitation at the rounds visits and other network meetings as well as between meetings. Facilitators work with host sites to prepare for visits and plan the network's professional learning (see chapter 7 for a more detailed description of the facilitator's role). They need a blend of knowledge and competencies, including knowledge of teaching and learning, skill and confidence in working with adult learners and facilitating meetings, familiarity with instructional rounds and the learning goals for each step, and credibility with network members. The more of these competencies they have at the outset, the better, but most of these skills can also be developed over time with training and ongoing support (which also require resources). In Iowa and Ohio, which are "networks of networks," with many facilitators, this support is an important part of the design.

A key consideration when choosing facilitators is what is the best blend of *insider* (members of the organization hosting the network, possibly staff people with time committed to this work) and *outsider* (people with clear outside affiliations, like universities, other partners, and consultants) for the role. As with most rounds network decisions, there is not one right answer, and there are trade-offs to consider.

Although several key insider roles could also be played by outsiders, some things are usually more convenient and cost-effective to be done internally—for example, membership maintenance, scheduling, and other organizational functions. Insiders are often also better at connecting rounds and the other work of the organization and at providing relevant context. The inside facilitators are generally not participants in the network, because of the time required to facilitate. What's more, the facilitator role and the participant role are different (figure 3.1). A good participant will not necessarily be a good facilitator.

Outsiders can provide skills, time, resources, and perspectives that insiders are less likely to have. An outsider may be more likely to notice (and to push) when network members' behavior defaults back to old patterns. Outsiders may also have access to knowledge—through a university, perhaps—that is not readily available to insiders. Outsiders can share with one network the practices that have developed in another, helping networks leapfrog in their own development. Additionally, an outsider can sometimes work in a system in a different way than an insider can. For example, a principal might be more likely to be candid about what she doesn't know in developing a problem of practice with a trusted outside facilitator than she might be if her deputy superintendent were the person helping her prepare for the visit. Outsiders may have more credibility and ability to push, especially on superintendents, compared with someone in the system. Outsiders need to help build the capacity of the network to do their work without defaulting into the role

---

FIGURE 3.1   DESCRIPTION OF FACILITATOR ROLE RESPONSIBILITIES

Facilitator/Coach Responsibilities for Instructional Rounds

Helping the rounds host figure out the problem of practice
- Session with principal and leadership team (or representatives of team)

Following up with the rounds host after the visit
- Session with principal and with leadership team
- Facilitate session with staff
- Prep time

Network sessions (no site visit)
- Rounds training session (Sept.)
- Training and planning session (May)
- Prep time

Instructional rounds sessions (site visits)
- Full-day sessions
- Prep time

Internal think tank meetings
- 40-80 minutes each
- Prep time (agenda, initial brainstorming)

Identifying and connecting external resources with specific content expertise as needed
- Prep time

Adapted with permission from Denny Buzzelli, Akron Public Schools

---

of "experts" on whom the networks rely as a way to avoid developing their own internal accountability and ownership of the work.

We encourage networks to have two cofacilitators, which gives the facilitators an opportunity to plan and learn together. Sharing the position also makes it easier to access the benefits of both insider and outsider roles.

A subtle resource a network needs in order to get started is the credibility to convene and host something like instructional rounds. Potential participants need to have the confidence, based on trust and reputation, that something good instructionally will come from a network sponsored by you and the other planners of your network. Engaging in instructional rounds is a leap of faith—many participants haven't ever experienced it and often have had bad experiences with things that on the surface looked like rounds. For an in-district network that will be working with teachers and administrators, you might benefit, as did Cambridge, from the active engagement of the union president. Union leaders served as key members of the rounds planning team in Ohio and stood side by side with district administrators at orientation sessions as some of the in-district networks were launched, answering questions and visibly lowering the anxieties of many teachers in the room. Networks also benefit from the inclusion of other respected thought leaders—as planners and early adopter members—in your community. These might be key superintendents at a state or regional level or key principals or teachers within a district. Consortium groups planning one or more network launches (like the AEA networks in Iowa or the multiple districts in Ohio) rely on the credibility of both the conveners and the participating members to give legitimacy to the work.

SETTING EXPECTATIONS AND NORMS

Your network will need to set expectations and norms, both around the mechanics of network practice—like time commitments and participant attendance policies—and for the deeper aspects of developing and supporting a network learning culture. Both are important to set the stage for a network that can support the structure as well as the culture of rounds well. Some things to consider in developing a learning culture include setting clear norms and expectations, creating a safe space for learning, helping people give honest feedback to one another, anchoring the work in the instructional core and theories of action, and creating mechanisms for continuous learning.

Establish Clear Expectations of What It Means to Be a Network Member

Expectations and norms are critical underpinnings of instructional rounds networks. While they will evolve and be revised by the network over time, some need to be established when launching the network. What commitments from its members does your network need if it is to accomplish its purposes? The Iowa networks, for instance (building on the work in Connecticut), specify expectations for attendance, active participation, willingness to be visited, confidentiality, honest communication, and mutual support and accountability (see exhibit A.3, Planning Template, in the appendix). In Ohio, the membership expectations were for districts—including the commitment of the superintendent to personally participate, the engagement of the mixed teams, a willingness to host a visit, a three-year commitment to the work, and financial commitments to defray the costs of visits. The Connecticut network reviews its norms and expectations annually, and the membership has made changes to reflect what the superintendents expect from each other. Last year, for example, members decided that two to three years before a network follow-up visit was too long. They decided that within a few months of a network visit, two superintendents would return for a mini-revisit to confer with the host superintendent and discuss the work she or he had done since the visit.

Despite the possibility of revising your expectations later, it is nevertheless important to identify them up front. For instance, earlier networks in Cambridge and Connecticut did not initially specify that participants had to *do something* back in their respective schools or districts. Theoretically, the participants could participate in rounds, learn from it personally, and contribute to the learning of their colleagues, and that would be enough. There are now clearer expectations for follow-up applications in Connecticut and Cambridge. On the other hand, the newer networks in Iowa and Ohio have benefited from this learning. For their members, the explicit expectations for some kind of follow-up have been clearer from the outset.

The trade-off with clear expectations, which can accelerate the impact of rounds, is that high expectations may make it harder to recruit members. One expectation that we never compromise on, however, is attendance. Rounds is not like another district meeting, where you might send a substitute who will keep track of the meeting details and report back to you later. Rounds is about learning, and—as we like to remind network members—a substitute can't do your learning for you.

Create a Safe Space for Learning

A rounds network has to be a safe space for personal learning, a place where educators can come and talk honestly about real issues that they face without feeling constrained in talking openly or doing anything that they might see as compromising themselves. Participating in rounds means taking risks and making yourself vulnerable. In many districts, these sessions are the first time that colleagues discuss teaching and leadership at this level of detail. Furthermore, network members are generally leaders who are expected to have answers. Under these circumstances, it can be hard for a leader to talk about what he or she doesn't know. This is particularly acute when there are mixed roles in the group. People may be reticent to admit gaps in knowledge or expose their confusion in front of someone who is their boss or whom they evaluate.

Examples of the challenges abound. In one network, for example, a new principal begged to be reassigned to a different small group when she found out she was assigned to the same group that her superintendent was in. In another network, it became clear that a superintendent (who did not have a strong instructional background) was uncomfortable observing and describing instruction alongside teachers from the district. Norms and protocols help create a safe space in situations like these.

The most important norm in instructional rounds is the norm of confidentiality—what the network sees and says stays in the network. Protocols shape the way people interact with each other. Groups benefit from simple structures that help them share air time, surface their different perspectives, and hear from everyone. The structures in protocols are not usually novel; their value comes from making the rules of interaction explicit—they establish that the group is accountable to each other and they provide the means for facilitators and participants to hold a group to their agreements. Protocols help people practice the skills they espouse but that they don't always know how to enact (we will discuss protocols in more detail later in the book).

Go Beyond the "Land of Nice"

Networks whose members feel safe but are not challenged to look at their practice and learn won't help scale up systems to support high-quality teaching and learning. Educators have a strong culture of being "nice" to each other. A facilitator involved in launching one of the Iowa networks described his biggest concern—that superintendents in his area would not be comfortable "saying anything unpleasant to one another." Others involved in networks have described how hard it is to shift from a culture characterized by the maxim, "If you don't have anything nice to say, don't say anything at all."

Successful networks use several complementary approaches to change this ingrained approach and the sets of beliefs underlying it. Protocols help. They provide people with alternative, verbal structures that set aside normal defaults. In addition, the careful, intense focus on staying in the descriptive voice is a powerful tool for focusing on what was actually said or done, not on the inferences and judgments triggered by the observation. Another key approach is to make it clear that the network is focusing on the personal learning of all its members, recognizing that their *practice* can be separated from who they are as *people* and can be improved. The tendency in schools and districts is to think about the individuals performing the work rather than the work itself. During rounds, the goal is to learn about *teaching*, not to focus on *teachers*. The work starts from the premise that good teaching (and good leading) is a set of professional practices that can be learned by most people. In order to support improvement, networks need to learn to recognize, name, and describe these practices—without being distracted by personality, style, or personal biases. Networks also need to make explicit that learning new ways of doing things is possible and comes with practice and effort.

Anchor the Work in the Instructional Core and Theories of Action

In the early stages of a network, the participants need to learn the rounds practice, understand the theoretical underpinnings of rounds (the instructional core and theories of action), and make connections to improving their systems. This is a lot to manage at once, and the tendency is to focus the most time and energy on learning the practice initially. This focus can be okay, but as you launch a network, keep in mind that the participants need to connect both the theory and their everyday practice in order for rounds to be more than interesting professional learning. The concepts of the instructional core and a theory of action help participants—who often operate in complex environments with multiple agendas and activities but little coherence—keep their conversation focused on what matters. The notion that if a school or district is engaged in improvement, you should be able to see its efforts reflected in its classrooms is a powerful common understanding that creates a tight link between theory and practice. A strong focus on problems of practice helps connect district improvement efforts with the teaching and learning conditions in the schools. A commitment to follow-up action—applying the ideas and approaches developed in the network—also ensures this connection.

Create Mechanisms for Continuous Learning

Launching helps networks get off to a good start, but it's the way networks learn and improve as they develop over time that determines what networks become. Setting up mechanisms to encourage feedback loops and process adjustments from the beginning makes it more likely that networks will create the time and space for reflection and revised action. Moreover, communication between members, especially if there is an expectation of work they have to do (participate in an annual reflection session, etc.), is improved. For example, the Connecticut network has a process for proposing norms, for collective decisions about enforcing them, and for reflection on whether to modify them. These discussions are data driven: For instance, an annual report on superintendent attendance over the year is given to the membership, which then decides what to do about any members who have missed too many sessions. There are similar reports on participation rates (in discussions, with frequency counts) used to check the norms of equal participation. The Cambridge and Ohio networks have think tanks that include a volunteer cross-section of the membership who help plan agendas, give feedback to the facilitators, and shape long-term planning for the networks. The Iowa networks are planning their evaluation process carefully from the beginning, devoting resources to it, determining the questions they are interested in answering, and figuring out how to gather data to answer those questions.

GETTING READY TO LAUNCH: ORIENTATION AND OTHER CONSIDERATIONS

The network serves as the foundation for the learning that will take place in rounds. By thinking carefully about convening, managing resources, and creating a learning culture, you are on the way to a powerful experience. The next chapters outline more of what rounds looks like, and as you read them, you may wish to return to this chapter to add nuance to your planning. Then again, there is only so much you can do ahead in convening, managing resources, and creating norms around learning. At some point, you have identified the membership, found a place to meet, clarified expectations, and you are ready to convene the first meeting of your network. Even if you don't feel ready, go for it. Remember, we learn to do the work by doing the work. A few practical suggestions about the actual launch of your network follow.

For starters, most networks do not just gather their membership together and show up in a school one morning. In addition to the preparation that needs to take place to set up the logistics and focus of the visit, the network needs to gather, get oriented as to why the members are here, go over ground rules, and, most importantly, practice the skills of observation and debriefing before imposing themselves on a school. This is typically done with a day-long orientation and visit simulation, using one or more classroom videos as a stand-in for the visits. The learning goals and a typical agenda for an orientation might look like those in figures 3.2 and 3.3.

FIGURE 3.2   EXAMPLE OF LEARNING GOALS FOR FIRST NETWORK LAUNCH MEETING

- Understand the importance of the instructional core
- Understand the steps of instructional rounds and the learning goals behind each step
- Develop skills in observing teaching and learning—describing what we see
- Develop skills in debriefing an observation
- Build relationships within the group

FIGURE 3.3   EXAMPLE OF AN AGENDA FOR FIRST NETWORK LAUNCH MEETING

- Welcome and Introductions
- Discussion of the instructional core (the only way that teaching and learning can improve is through changes in the relationship of students and teachers in the presence of content)
- Network rounds overview and questions (what a typical visit looks like, what rounds is and is not, how it differs from walkthroughs or forms of supervision used in this setting)
- Hopes and fears; developing norms (after discussion of hopes and fears, the group works together to set norms to maximize the chances of their hopes being realized and to minimize the possibility of their fears coming true)
- The discipline of seeing (examples and introduction of key skills needed to develop the distinctive approach to observation—descriptive, nonjudgmental, detailed—that is used in rounds)
- Observation practice (includes one or more classroom video clips—usually about 20 minutes each, with participants taking notes as if they were in a classroom)
- Debriefing: description, analysis, prediction and the next level of work (this continues the simulation portion, and is conducted to match what would be done as part of a typical visit)
- Reflection (an opportunity to reflect on and improve the day's experience, to cycle back to earlier discussions about purpose and connection of rounds to instructional improvement at the core, and to share observations of what participants noticed about how they learned during the day, individually and collectively)

∎

Tips and Takeaways

As you move forward in forming and launching your rounds network, a few points are worth emphasizing:

- *Think from the beginning about how you will learn and improve the rounds practice.* Most of the ideas in this chapter represent initial decisions to get your network launched. As you focus on them, however, keep in mind the importance of continuous learning and improvement for individuals and the network. Throughout the book, you will read more about the networks we have worked with, and you will see powerful stories of evolution and learning—within and across networks. These don't happen by accident. Think about how you will design the mechanisms for that continuous learning—whether it is through the use of opening and closing calibrations, think tanks, data-based network sessions, plus/delta exercises at the end of visits, or reflective retreats. The more you can build continuous improvement into the fabric of your network, the more likely you are to develop a network that supports you in getting to your goals.

- *Encourage public learners.* The presence and active participation of public learners—highly respected authority figures who are publicly open about their learning—is key to a successful learning network. Although these behaviors are somewhat emergent (and their appearance cannot be controlled or predicted), successful networks can invite participants with this in mind and can position public learners for visibility when they emerge—like having them host early rounds visits. Facilitators and others can comment favorably on the public learners, the risks these respected people are taking, and what they are modeling. In doing so, these commentators reflect back to the group how valuable this behavior is.

- *Keep the purpose in mind.* Setting up the network and, indeed, conducting rounds are not ends in themselves, but means to helping districts and schools make large-scale improvements in the instructional core to best serve the learning of all students. Network functioning and learning need to be tuned and calibrated to district improvement efforts and help contribute to them in a focused and coherent way. If rounds is just another activity among the many that districts engage in, then much of the effort of the network will be wasted.

- *It is not just what you do, but how you do it that matters.* While there are strong structural implications for each of the suggestions in this chapter (e.g., the need for facilitators and mechanisms for customizing), there is also a powerful cultural overlay for all of them. It is not just a question of hiring a facilitator; it is how the facilitation is done to empower participants and to engage them in the work (and not have them passively listen to "experts" or authority figures on how to teach or how to conduct rounds). A key part of what your network is doing is building trust and collective efficacy. You will know that you are successful when individual participants publicly acknowledge they don't know something and let down their guard and take risks with one another; when members take ownership of the norms and enforce them; and when pressure for pushing and deepening the work comes from network members, not outsiders or facilitators.

- *When in doubt, let the network figure it out.* A corollary to the preceding point is that a large part of the "how" is letting the network do the work. The conveners have to name a few things early on to get things going, but they do not have to decide everything—nor should they. Much is new and unknown when networks are being launched, and for most people, the natural response to such uncertainty is to impose more structure. For instructional rounds, that response does not help the network develop its professional practice. If you put participants' urgent questions back to them, they will figure out how to answer their own questions and design the structures they need. In essence, they will start to become a real network.

When these preparation and implementation suggestions are enacted, networks have enormous power to unlock peer learning, to connect theory to on-the-ground action, and to support improvement in the instructional core through rounds. The networks provide a place to develop a shared and discussable practice as a key ingredient in professionalizing leadership and teaching and in supporting educators in improving instruction for all students.

CHAPTER 4

Learning to See,
Unlearning to Judge

The new network group was excited. The members had read articles, spoken with colleagues who had been doing rounds, and thought the process had real potential for helping them improve learning and teaching in their schools. They had committed one day a month to each other, and today was their orientation day. After observing a video of a middle school math class, four of them debriefed the observation in a small group.

"I noticed that the teacher was well prepared," said Rebecca.

"There was a clear agenda on the board, but I didn't see any objectives," said Thomas.

"I was bored just watching that class," said Walter. "It reminded me why I never liked math."

"Well, I'm not really a math person," said Catalina, "but the kids really didn't look engaged to me."

"Yup, it's obvious why this country struggles with middle school math scores," said Thomas.

"I didn't think it was that bad," said Rebecca. "We only saw a little of the lesson—I think we need to give the teacher the benefit of the doubt."

The facilitator gathered a few observations from the whole group and then started the second video.

Like many educators who form instructional rounds networks, Rebecca, Thomas, Walter, and Catalina each have an idea about what they want to see when they walk into a classroom. They have rich experience as teachers and as supporters and evaluators of teachers. They think they're ready to start rounds, but they're not quite ready. What's obvious to one isn't obvious to all, and while several share a sense of concern about what they saw, it's not clear that they're concerned about the same thing. They move quickly to judgment and their own experiences and conclusions. They don't know how to slow down the snap-judgment part of themselves and simply describe what they have seen. They also don't know why they should bother describing at all. And that is why they are spending their first day developing some common practice and language that they will continue to develop together over time.

The discipline of description is the core practice on which rounds are based and is quite novel and counterintuitive for most educators. It must be learned, and some other habits—like using general or judgmental language or jargon—must be unlearned. Educators tend not to be very good at observing classrooms. And why should they be? Teachers usually have very limited experience observing classrooms, since the bulk of their time is spent in their own classroom, teaching. Principals and other administrators may have more experience observing multiple classrooms, but usually with the purpose of evaluating teachers. The kind of observing we're talking about here focuses not on teachers themselves but on the teaching, learning, and content of the instructional core. What is the task that students are working on? In what specific ways are the teacher and students interacting in relation to the task? By *description*, we mean the evidence of what you see—not what you think about what you see. Figure 4.1 provides examples of description and the more common language of judgment. Take the example, "Fast-paced." If the observer were pushed to explain what led her to that conclusion, she might say, "Every time the teacher moved to a new problem, I counted at least five students who were still working on the earlier problem." There's the description—the judgment-free evidence—that allows colleagues to decide whether they'd consider the lesson fast-paced.

Administrators often have to unlearn their well-honed skill of deciding rather quickly what a teacher needs to work on and instead take off their evaluating glasses and look with fresh eyes to see what is happening in and across classrooms. Those who are unlearning need to be convinced that it makes sense to let go of their habits, assumptions, and competence in this area in order to try on a different way of approaching what goes on in classrooms. Most educators have little experience

---

FIGURE 4.1   EXAMPLES OF JUDGMENTAL AND NONJUDGMENTAL DESCRIPTION

Description Includes Observer's Judgment

- Fast-paced.
- Too much time on discussion, not enough time on individual work.
- Excellent classroom management.
- Teacher used effective questioning techniques with a range of students.
- Teacher read from a book that was not at the appropriate level for the class.
- Teacher had good rapport with students.
- Students conducted a very sophisticated lab experiment.

Description Without Judgment

- Teacher asks, "How did you figure out this problem?" Student explains.
- Students followed directions in the text to make circuit boards.
- Teacher said, "Write the words that I spell in the blank spaces. S-P-O-T. D-O-T. P-O-T."
- Task: Find different ways to create a total of 31.

  Student 1 wrote in math journal:
  $$5+5+5+5+5+5+1 = 31$$
  $$10+10+10+1 = 31$$
  S2: $20+9 = 03$
  S3: $41-10 = 31$
  $$2+3 \times 3+16 = 31$$

- Student 1 asks student 2: "What are we supposed to write down?"
  Student 2: "I don't know."

---

with starting a conversation strictly from evidence, so almost everyone needs help with that skill. For those who are unlearning, it is particularly challenging. It is also doable and essential for the rounds practice.

Classroom observation in the network rounds model is a discipline—a *practice*, in the sense that it is a pattern of ways of observing and talking and is designed to create a common understanding among a group of practitioners about the nature of their work. A central part of that practice is deciding in advance *what* to observe, *how* to observe, and, most importantly, *how to talk about what is seen.* This chapter examines why it's so essential to be descriptive, what it looks like in practice, and how to develop the network's observation capabilities.

WHY BE DESCRIPTIVE?

Why focus initially on description? The basic reason is that we are searching for cause-and-effect relationships between what we observe teachers and students doing and what students actually know and are able do as a consequence. If we start by arguing about our assessments of what we see, then we seldom get to actually describing and predicting the causal relationship between teaching and learning. We end up debating our preconceptions about what constitutes good instruction, rather than analyzing what we see going on in classrooms. This is a bit like doctors discussing whether a patient is healthy without identifying vital signs, or like lawyers discussing whether someone is guilty without assembling facts, or like carpenters discussing whether a house looks sturdy without describing the construction materials and joints. Such discussions generate lots of heat without much light. If we start with a common evidentiary basis, there is still room for debate and different diagnoses later on, and we are operating from a more visible starting point than individual beliefs and assumptions.

The idea that instruction is at the core of school improvement is typically not a particularly hard sell with educators in this period of high-stakes accountability. Practitioners tend to agree—at least at the aspirational level—that they should be concerned about the quality of instruction in the classroom. A tougher part of the problem, in our experience and in the experience of many others who are working to improve instruction, is getting people to agree on *what* they are actually looking for in the classroom and translating that agreement into specific guidance and action for educators. This is where the discipline of classroom observation gets difficult. The first thing that educators discover when they attempt to observe is that they have very different ideas about what they are looking for in classroom practice and that these ideas are based on assumptions that are usually not discussed. Too often, our first instinct when we approach a classroom is to look for what is "good" or "bad" about what we see, without examining what causes us to make this judgment.

To talk with each other productively about what we see in classrooms, we have to back up a step or two from where we usually start and simply try to observe what we see at the most basic descriptive level—without the heavy judgmental overlay that we typically bring to classroom observations—and develop a common language for describing what we see. For educators, this basic step is the most difficult part of learning how to improve instruction. We tend to be passionate about our beliefs about what constitutes good teaching and learning, and to forgo our evaluative impulses is an unnatural act.

The *ladder of inference* can be helpful in providing both an image and a language for discussing what it means to stay in the descriptive.[1] The bottom rung of the ladder is description. As you move up the ladder, you get farther from the evidence and closer to your beliefs, assumptions, and conclusions. If you start at the top of the ladder, it's hard to go back down—the other rungs are missing. If you start at the bottom of the ladder and work your way up—and you do need to go up eventually to get to recommendations for improvement—then it is easier to go back up and down, to check assumptions and beliefs, and to be clear about what the recommendations are intended to address.

The discipline of description is helpful when you're operating on your own, because it slows you down and helps you identify what your conclusion is based on, allowing you to check your assumptions before and after taking action. Sometimes, your assumptions are so strong that you look for what you expect and your assumptions subtly alter what you see. When you discipline yourself to stay in the descriptive mode, you are likely to notice more accurately what is happening in the classroom and your inferences will be on a firmer evidentiary foundation. While description is helpful when you're alone, it's imperative when you're engaging with others. At the heart of rounds is dialogue. Comments that start at the top of the ladder impede conversation and keep instructional rounds an individual rather than collective practice.

For example, in our work in schools, we often hear statements like "Teachers have high expectations for students" or "Students were confused" or "That was a really great lesson." These statements are problematic as a basis for understanding and improving teaching and learning for a number of reasons.

First, we probably have very different pictures of what "high expectations" or "confused" or "great" looks like. We might use the same language that another observer uses, but we might not mean the same thing. This reinforces our tendency to assume that shared language means shared belief, which is a dangerous assumption unless the shared language is grounded in shared evidence and dialogue. When we assume we mean the same thing, we usually stop discussing it, which closes us off to varied perspectives and potential learning and leaves us each to proceed in individual directions (which usually translates into different actions).

Second, what I think is high expectations in the particular case we observed, you might think is a high volume of work but not intellectually demanding work, or is something better suited for fourth grade than ninth grade. We see the same thing, but draw different conclusions. If we assembled the evidence, we could debate the evidence and then work together to decide what it means in terms of student learning.

Third, as soon as you say "great," I'm likely to either nod in agreement or stay quiet if I disagree —but either way, we don't have anything to talk about, because we haven't named what's happening in the instructional core. Words like *good*, *great*, *weak*, *bad*—judgment words—are conversation stoppers. When we rely on judgments, we have not shared the evidentiary basis for our analysis, which makes it hard to disagree because it sounds like a personal challenge if a colleague says, "I didn't think that was great." It's not about whether it was great or we liked it—it's about understanding the teaching and whether it's producing the kind of learning we want.

WHAT IT LOOKS LIKE IN PRACTICE: LEARNING AND UNLEARNING

Like other skills, learning to see and hear the particulars of teaching practice requires practice. Like a muscle, it gets stronger with repetition and practice. The best way to strengthen the observation muscle is to observe lots of classrooms. When we are learning to see, we start off with three questions rooted in the instructional core:

1. What are teachers doing and saying?
2. What are students doing and saying?
3. What is the task?

As you get more sophisticated in your observations and link your observations to a particular problem of practice that the host school and district would like feedback about, the questions become more specific, but ultimately, the questions are variations on these three that center on the instructional core. A simpler form of the questions is "What do you see?" That question focuses on the descriptive, rather than other questions that are implicitly running through your head, like "What do you want to see?" "What don't you see?" "What do you think about what you see?" "Do you like being in this classroom?"

When they ask us to share our observational protocols, people are usually surprised, and a bit disappointed, that we don't give them a detailed set of prescriptions for how to identify "high-quality instruction." Their response is typically, "Is that all there is?" The answer is yes. The discipline of observation inheres not in the complexity or sophistication of the protocol, but in the *focus* of the observation and in the laser-like emphasis on the cause-and-effect relationship between what we observe teachers and students doing and what students actually know and can consequently do. A simple protocol makes it easier to describe the relationship between what we observe in classrooms and the predicted consequences for student learning.

Fortunately, there is a relatively easy antidote to the common plight of leaping to the top rungs of the ladder of inference. Judgments are usually based on something, even when you're not sure what that basis is. The antidote is a simple question that prods you to peel back your judgments: "What's the evidence?" That is, "What evidence did you see that made you think . . . [there were high expectations]?" This question will produce descriptive answers like "the assignment was to write a personal memoir and revise it three times." A follow-up revision to the statement "Students were confused" might be "Three students asked whether it mattered what letter you used in a variable expression." Another version of this question is: "What did you see or hear that made you think that?"

Participants are likely to need coaching in this area. The coach is often the facilitator, but there could be other experienced observers in the group who teach the group what it means to stick to description, and to model pushing for evidence. The sidebar "'What's the Evidence?' Ball Game" shows one way we have helped coach groups.

We have played the "What's the Evidence?" ball game in groups ranging from eight to fifty people. In small groups, we usually continue until each person has shared at least one piece of evidence. In large groups, we continue until we've had at least a couple examples of pushing and a few examples of description. This game makes people's observation public while combining it with fun and the collective ownership of language.

Using video before going into classrooms can be very helpful because everyone is seeing the same instruction (whereas only four people might see a classroom together at a given time during actual rounds) and can talk about it as a common "text." Also, if you watch video of classrooms outside the school or district that you'll be visiting, it's a bit easier to separate people and practice initially, because

---

"WHAT'S THE EVIDENCE?" BALL GAME

Watch a short (approximately ten-minute) video clip of a classroom, using the three core questions (What are teachers doing and saying? What are students doing and saying? What is the task?) or the one essential question (What do you see?).

Tell people to take notes on those questions. After the video, give them a couple of minutes to turn and talk with a neighbor about what evidence they have seen. This opportunity to talk helps people be ready to say something when the ball comes to them during the game. Invite people to stand up. Before you throw the ball for the first time, explain that you and the others are going to help each other build your descriptive muscle. Whoever has the ball shares a piece of evidence. If the group thinks the statement has an opinion or a judgment in it, the group is going to say, "What's the evidence?" The person with the ball tries again. If the group thinks it still needs tuning, the group repeats, "What's the evidence?" This continues until the group is satisfied, at which point the person throws the ball to a colleague. Practice having the group ask, "What's the evidence?" together before you start the game. The coach might need to help the group sometimes by pointing out opportunities to push with language like, "Did that sound like evidence to you? . . . What did you think about that? . . . Are you going to let her get away with that?" and so forth. The coach may also need to help tune the language when a participant is stuck or open it up for the group to help, "Let's peel this back. How might we say this using descriptive-only language?"

---

you don't have to think so much about the reaction of someone in the room to your observations and can focus on the discipline itself (see the appendix for video resources).

Sometimes, we enlist group members to help coach by asking people to serve as "Evidence Police." These people have the responsibility for enforcing an evidence-only rule in their group. Eventually, it will become part of the group's practice, so that everyone will call each other on it, but even in experienced groups, the pull to the Black Hole of Opinions is quite strong. For this reason, we find it helpful to designate specific people to listen carefully for violations of evidence-only. If they hear something that sounds as if it might be up the ladder of inference, they ask "What's the evidence?" or "What did you see or hear that made you think that?" to help their colleagues back down the ladder.

We nominate people in a semirandom way (e.g., the person with the longest last name or whose first name is alphabetically first in a small group) for this role rather than asking for volunteers because in education's "Land of Nice," being "nice" to each other is equated with not challenging each other. The rounds network will push hard against this improvement-impeding norm over time, but initially requires careful creation of the space, authority, and expectation for people to push each other. Designating Evidence Police makes it easier for the enforcer to push and for colleagues to be pushed—someone is playing a role, not in her or his typical role of Sally the principal or Fred the teacher or Carlos the superintendent. This helps separate people and practice, a distinction that rounds continually tries to reinforce. People usually enjoy the role of enforcer and take their responsibility seriously, but just because they have been nominated doesn't mean they're good at it. Not surprisingly, having the longest last name or a first name that starts with "A" does not make one an instant expert in sticking to description. It just means you're paying special attention to it and the group has given you the authority to gently call people on violations of it with the question of "What's the evidence?"

Many people will be skeptical about the value of sticking to evidence, so it's worth having an explicit conversation about it. After an observation, discuss what people noticed about observation and sticking to evidence. Was it hard? What was the point of sticking to the evidence? What insight did you gain from this process? For example, if someone said, "Positive classroom climate," or "The teacher was prepared," or "That was a low-level lesson," what was the effect of those words? Facilitators can make the point that we often have different ideas of what "low-level" means, and we have to unpack that and get more specific to have a common conversation about what was happening in the classroom. Did people notice things other than what you noticed? How are your observations connected to what you value in instruction?

We find that the ladder of inference is helpful for people as a touchstone. Once it's introduced into the network's lexicon, people say things like "That comment was pretty far up the ladder," or "I know I'm way up the ladder of inference here, . . ." This latter comment is usually followed by the conclusion or judgment that the person really didn't want to suppress "but I just have to say . . ."—but at least the speaker recognizes the lack of evidence, which then makes it easier to follow up with some description.

We also find that even experienced networks need refreshers on this core practice of description, particularly if network members haven't seen each other for a while (students aren't the only ones whose practice gets a bit ragged over the summer!). Additionally, in small groups, people tend to be less vigilant or willing to call each other on judgmental language than in large groups. One tactic that can help is to give each person a colored card (e.g., a yellow index card) to hold up when he or she hears judgment. Some people find this visual reminder easier than a verbal one. We've also seen facilitators direct groups to hum when they hear non-evidence-based comments. Since humming is fairly anonymous, this can be a low-risk way for beginning groups to practice pushing each other in a friendly way.

IT'S DESCRIPTIVE, BUT IS IT USEFUL?

Sometimes people get stuck on what we mean by evidence. Is it just any fact? Is "students are sitting on the rug" evidence? By *evidence*, we mean descriptive statements of what you see. These descriptive statements are critical because they give us a common basis for our conversation. They open the door to conversation rather than close it. However, not all forms of evidence are equally valuable. Even if the conversation stays in the descriptive mode, some kinds of evidence are more helpful than others.

Consider the examples in figure 4.2. What are the general characteristics of the data in the rows? What distinguishes the examples in the first row from those in the second? Which would you find more helpful, and why?

We use examples and questions like these when working with networks to surface the idea of grain size, or how specific the description is. The term *grain size* comes from, among other places, photography in the era when cameras used only film. The corresponding term for digital photography is now *noise*. When a photograph is taken under conditions of very low light, with a very fast film (or high ISO), you get a very fuzzy, grainy picture with low resolution around the components of the images. Sometimes fuzzy is beautiful; sometimes it's not. When an image is fuzzy, the grain size is large. It may be hard to distinguish the elements in the photograph. As conditions change, the amount of light available for the image grows, the edges get sharper within the image, and the noise or graininess of the image decreases. So we speak of evidence as having large, medium, or small grain size—that is, of being fuzzy or sharp. The smaller the grain size, the clearer the picture of what is happening in a classroom.

In general, finer-grained descriptions (like those in the second row) make it easier for us to discuss classrooms and to build a common picture of what is happening

---

FIGURE 4.2   LARGE-GRAINED AND FINE-GRAINED EVIDENCE

Large-Grained Evidence

- Lesson on the four main causes of the Civil War.
- Teacher questions students about the passage they just read.
- Students practicing higher-order thinking skills.
- Teacher introduced the concept of fractions and had students apply the concept in a hands-on activity.
- Teacher checked frequently for comprehension.
- Teacher made curriculum relevant to students' lives.

Fine-Grained Evidence

- Teacher: "How are volcanoes and earthquakes similar and different?"
- Teacher: "Boys and girls, today's number is 30. Who can give me a string of numbers that go up to 30?"
- Prompt for student essays: "What role did symbolism play in foreshadowing the main character's dilemma?"
- Students worked individually even though they were in groups. Each worked on own paper and didn't talk with others.
- Students made up questions about the book they'd just read.

---

in classrooms. We refer to more general comments (like those in the first row) as "boulders." It might seem that we could build our understanding more quickly with boulders—"The teacher asked a lot of questions," "Students were doing a hands-on activity," and so on—but this is a shaky foundation. The more general the description is, the more room there is for fuzziness or interpretation and the more general our predictions and thinking about the next level of work tend to be. Statements like "Teacher: 'How are volcanoes and earthquakes similar and different?'" are more helpful than "Teacher questions students about the passage they just read" because they help you predict what students in the classroom will be able to do—that is, compare and contrast. If you only knew that the teacher was questioning students, you wouldn't know whether those questions were asking students to recall information, understand, analyze, or evaluate, each of which has different implications for what students would be able to do, and different implications for what the next level of work would be. There is nothing inherently wrong with the examples in the top row (remember, we are trying to get away from thinking of things as good or bad and instead are thinking about them as a practice, which applies to our own work as well as what we see in classrooms), but they will be less helpful in the rounds process. Pebbles are the building blocks of improvement. As with observing through evidence, the more explicit you are about what levels of evidence are most helpful in conversation, the more quickly you will refine your instructional rounds.

The conversation about what is most helpful will probably surface a few other things that commonly crop up when people are learning the discipline of description. Sometimes, people are working so hard to stick with evidence or are so nervous about being "wrong" that they pick something safe to share, like "Students are sitting on the rug." Yes, that is an example of evidence—but is it useful evidence? It's only helpful if it helps you understand something about the instructional core in that classroom. A follow-up question might be, "How is that relevant for what was happening in that classroom?" A participant might say, "Well, students listened quietly while the teacher read a book aloud." A follow-up to that might be, "How did you know they were listening?" to which a participant might say, "When the teacher paused and asked students to predict what would happen next, several students raised their hands." A colleague might add, "I noticed that five girls and three boys raised their hands, and the teacher called on one of the boys." And so on.

Another common phenomenon is that people talk about what they *don't* see. We call this "the dog that didn't bark." Here are a few examples: "There were no objectives on the board." "The teacher didn't call on anyone who wasn't raising their hand." "The teacher didn't ask follow-up questions." These statements tell something about the speaker's picture of what an effective classroom looks like, but tell little about what was actually happening in the observed classroom. We encourage people to describe, as much as possible, what they see, not what they don't see. Sometimes this requires a simple reframing: "The teacher only called on students with raised hands." "The pattern of questioning was teacher asks a question, student answers, teacher moves on to a new question." Sometimes this means asking why this seems important. Does it matter that there were no objectives? What was the evidence that the students were clear on the purpose of the lesson? The list of what you don't see could be infinitely long and doesn't typically help the group deepen its understanding of what causes learning.

The final common thing that happens when people are learning to see is that some people don't take written notes during observations, which makes it a lot harder to talk about fine-grained evidence later on. We have learned that it helps to explicitly tell people to take notes and to show them what it looks like. It's more demanding to take notes than not to; thus, it helps to make the expectation clear. Some people aren't sure what to write. We address this issue of uncertainty by sharing our own practice of what our notes look like and what we tend to focus on in a classroom.

Beyond the three core questions (What are teachers doing and saying? What are students doing and saying? What is the task?), our focus in a classroom is informed by both the host problem of practice (more on this in chapter 5) and the lenses we bring to the work. Some people pay special attention to what's on the walls, some always look for objectives, and some hone in on particular students and watch their participation (e.g., students of color, boys, students sitting by themselves). And just as in any note-taking situation, we all have different ways of taking notes. It's helpful to be explicit about all of these things in the network.

Here's our short list of what we tend to zoom in on when we're observing in classrooms. Your list may be different. We're not offering this as the right way, but as an example. The four of us look at slightly different things, but we're also consistent about a few of them.

- First, we get ourselves oriented to the classroom. What grade is it? What content area? How many students are there? How many girls? How many boys? How many adults are there? How many minutes into the class are we? It takes us about a minute to note these facts.
- Then we look at the task. What are students being asked to do? What are they actually doing?
- We also look at patterns of interaction. Is it teacher-student-teacher? Do students talk with each other? Do students initiate conversation, or are they always responding to the teacher?
- We listen to questions. What questions are being asked? Who's asking them? What are the responses to the questions?
- We consider time. How much time is spent on what activity? We also note time periodically throughout the observation as part of mapping what we see.

One of the ways we're explicit about note-taking is to share our own notes. We do this by taking notes on an overhead or another projectable format while watching a video and then showing the actual notes to network participants while talking through what we wrote and didn't write and why. Or, during a network meeting, we take notes as people are engaged in an activity and then we share those notes. In some ways, this variation is closer to a classroom observation in all its messiness— moving around trying to hear small group conversations, capturing directions, and seeing what people wrote down as evidence of the task. We have found that partici- pants are quite reassured to see that even with all the practice we've had, we don't capture everything, we start sentences we don't finish, and we're a bit messy.

For many people, the nuances of what kinds of description are more and less helpful won't make sense until they are more deeply into the rounds process and are really trying to use them. As one network participant said, "I didn't really understand how important it was to have fine-grained evidence until after our first rounds visit. Now I'm taking much better notes. I know I have a long way to go, but I think I'm starting to get it."

■

Tips and Takeaways

Besides learning new approaches, observation requires that many of us unlearn some things. Often, unlearning is harder than learning. Here are a few tips to keep in mind:

- *Discomfort is okay.* Seeing, hearing, and discussing the rich and varied life of classrooms is often most frightening for the people who are sup- posed to be leading the work of improvement. Will I lose all credibility as the [superintendent, principal, coach, master teacher, etc.] if I some- how expose that I don't know everything about teaching and learning? This worry often propels people to make evaluative pronouncements about what they've seen out of a desire to prove their expertise. One of the beautiful things about a network of colleagues focused on improve- ment is that the very source of the angst is also what makes it such a rich source of learning and reassurance for the participants. Opening up our own practice, vulnerabilities, questions, and ideas and discussing them with colleagues shows us that we are not so very different. It shows us that together, we are and can become a lot smarter than if we each tried to think about and improve teaching and learning on our own. Nevertheless, this work is scary before it's energizing and catalytic. One way to make it a little less scary is to acknowledge up front that this is challenging and, for most of us, unfamiliar work; that we wouldn't expect anyone to know it, no matter what their role is; and that we will all get better at it together. And then it's okay to let people squirm a bit, because there is often good learning that comes out of discomfort.

- *Be hard-nosed about evidence-only right from the beginning.* The number one challenge for most people is staying in the descriptive mode—this persists over time as a challenge and is particularly difficult at the beginning of the network's work together. The best remedy for this is practice, practice, practice, and being vigilant about calling each other on it when veering away from the descriptive. Participants will be tempted to let a few non-evidentiary comments go unchecked. Resist the temptation. You are not doing your colleagues, your network, and, ultimately, your students, a favor by letting the conversation be undisciplined. Once a few judgments slip into the conversation, they have a habit of reproducing like rabbits. Early intervention will help to establish a norm for how you talk with each other and will help to develop a practice of observation that is evidence-based and will later be a critical foundation for instructional improvement.

- *Discuss the why behind description.* The number two challenge, which is related to the number one challenge, is convincing people why it's important to stay in the descriptive. Some people will accept that this is part of the practice, or they trust the facilitator or leader who says it's important, and that's reason enough to do it. Other people will be convinced that they can walk into a classroom and in three minutes be able to diagnose what is going on and what the teacher needs to do. Folks in the latter category will have little patience for the process of collective observation and dialogue, and bringing them on board can be a slow process of the group's reinforcing the norms of description and one-on-one conversations about why it's important. These people are usually questioning many parts of rounds—the network, the description, the time it takes, its connection to results—and will need both conversation and experience to discover that rounds is different from what they're used to and how it can be powerful in their work. Many people will fall in between—they're willing to try it, but they don't really get why it matters. For both the questioners and the in-betweeners, having explicit conversations about why it matters, with specific examples of evidence and judgment and the kinds of conversations you can have, will help. And then you need to get into classrooms and go through the whole process of rounds, where it will become more apparent how evidence serves as a foundation.

- *Keep track of what you're learning about description, and revisit it over time.* As we discussed in chapter 3, part of how the network develops is to keep track of its learning over time. Description is a good place to start practicing that, particularly because it needs to be revisited and reinforced periodically, no matter how expert the network is. Networks might start by keeping a short list of tips that they build over their first few practice sessions, like "no judgments; small grain size; focus on what you see, not what you don't see; must be relevant," and so forth.

Even though it can feel slow at the beginning to focus so much on description, this is an example of "go slow to go fast." In courses we teach at Harvard and with practitioners, we spend many hours watching video and describing what we see before allowing people to move to analysis, prediction, and the next level of work. Educators may feel that they have neither the time nor the patience to spend hours on description, but we all still need lots of practice. This doesn't mean that networks should hold off on classroom visits until every participant has mastered description. After a few practice sessions, it's time to go into classrooms. Networks continue to work on description intensely during the first months of visits and revisit these lessons regularly. If you build a strong foundation, you will be able to accelerate the network's learning and application of that learning to improvement in instruction.

CHAPTER 5

Doing Rounds Part 1:
Problem of Practice and Observing

There was a buzz in the room as rounds was about to begin. Principal Randall Lewis stood at the front of the library, where the network had gathered for coffee, muffins, and conversation before the official start to the day. "Welcome to Jefferson Middle School. We're excited to have you here today to help us with our problem of practice. We're also a little nervous. Well, maybe a lot nervous, but that's okay. We're proud of our school, and we know we have a lot of work to do. I've told the teachers that this is about my learning and the network's learning, and that we're going to get lots of good information from having so many eyes and ears in our classrooms."

Randall asked his colleagues to take out the handout in their folders describing current school and district initiatives. "In the spring of last year, we rolled out a new literacy initiative that has required a radical shift in teaching strategies for many of our teachers. A year later, we're trying to understand what we've learned and what we haven't yet mastered and whether it's translating into different kinds of learning for students." After Randall described the problem of practice, he pointed group members to their schedules to learn which observation team they would join and where they would visit: "The classroom numbering in the school is quite creative, so if you get lost, your best bet is to ask a student."

The participants gathered their belongings, grabbed a school map and observation schedule in one hand and some paper for taking notes in the other, and found and greeted the other members of their observation team. There was a sense of anticipation—much like a group of scientists about to embark on field work for data collection.

After a network has prepared itself by learning about the instructional core and theories of action, launching a network, and developing the discipline of seeing, it is time to engage in the practice of rounds. It is time to go into schools and classrooms. In this chapter and the next chapter, we describe a "typical" rounds cycle and its related learning goals. Although each network has put its own stamp on the rounds process, there is a set of common elements that are consistent across all instructional rounds networks: a problem of practice; observation of practice; observation debrief; and the next level of work. Adding an element into the mix could still remain true to the rounds model. Taking out any one of the four elements, however, would no longer constitute rounds. These elements of the rounds practice are summarized in table 5.1. This chapter elaborates on the first two element of rounds: identifying the problem of practice and observing the practice.

Rounds has two primary learning goals that inform each other:

1. Build skills of network members by coming to a common understanding of effective practice and how to support it.
2. Support instructional improvement at the host site (school or district) by sharing what the network learns and by building skills at the local level.

Especially in the early development of a network, many network participants primarily focus on the second of these two goals—how can we help the people who are hosting the visit? This is a laudable and important goal, but it is not the only goal. Rounds visits help the network develop as a group that, over time, builds a rich sense of what they hope to see in classrooms, agreement about what they are actually seeing, and strategies for how to make the hope the reality. Rounds also helps all the individuals in the network, whether they are the host of a visit or a colleague participating in the visit, sharpen their understanding of the instructional core and their personal theory of action about their role in improving it. If rounds does not meet all these goals, the network won't last long. It takes a lot of time and energy to participate in rounds, and if the only benefit were to the host, that would probably not be enough to sustain participants, especially since in most networks, each participant only hosts once every two or three years. More often, rounds does meet all these goals, but sometimes participants aren't aware of how much they're learning, since their focus tends to be outward rather than inward. There are multiple ways to help participants focus both outward and inward, as we describe in this chapter and later in the book.

TABLE 5.1   THE FOUR ELEMENTS OF ROUNDS

Problem of Practice	Observation of Practice	Observation Debrief	Next Level of Work
School identifies a problem of practice that ■ focuses on the instructional core; ■ is directly observable; ■ is actionable (is within the school/district's control and can be improved in real time); ■ connects to a broader strategy of improvement (school, system). ■ Network adopts the problem of practice as the focus for the network's learning.	Observation teams collect data that is ■ descriptive not evaluative; ■ specific; ■ about the instructional core; ■ related to the problem of practice.	Observation teams discuss the data: ■ *Describe* what you saw. ■ *Analyze* the descriptive evidence (What patterns do you see? How might you group the data?). ■ *Predict* what students are learning. If you were a student in this class/school and you did everything the teacher told you to do, what would you know and be able to do?	Brainstorm the next level of work: ■ Share district-level theory of action. ■ Share district context, including resources, professional development, and current initiatives. ■ Brainstorm the next level of work for this week/next month/by the end of the year. ■ Brainstorm suggestions for school level and for district level. ■ Tie suggestions to the district's (and school's) theory of action.
Additional Steps to Support This Element of Rounds			
Provide school- or district-level context for the problem of practice. Describe optimal teaching and learning in relation to this problem of practice: ■ What would students be doing/saying? ■ What would teachers be doing/saying? ■ Create a working draft that captures the ongoing development of the group's learning.	May include a specific format for observation note-taking or a set of guidelines: ■ What are students doing/saying? ■ What are teachers doing/saying? ■ What is the task?	Use affinity protocol to group the data. Use external standards to group the data.	Ask additional questions: ■ What do teachers need to know to support optimal learning (described in the working draft)? ■ What does the school/district need to know to support optimal learning? ■ Build a working draft of what optimal leading and learning look like at the school and district level (What are teachers, principals, and central office administrators saying/doing?).

PROBLEM OF PRACTICE

The first step in rounds is to identify a problem of practice that the network will focus on during the rounds visit. A rich problem of practice

- focuses on the instructional core;
- is directly observable;
- is actionable (is within the school's or district's control and can be improved in real time);
- connects to a broader strategy of improvement (school, system);
- is high-leverage (if acted on, it would make a significant difference for student learning).

In short, the problem of practice is something that you care about that would make a difference for student learning if you improved it. The problem of practice is a critical component of rounds for several reasons: It helps focus the attention of the network—"Of all the things we could pay attention to in classrooms, we're going to focus particularly on [questions, task, talk, etc]." It also helps make it more likely that the visit will be fruitful learning for both the hosts and the network participants. We have repeatedly found that problems of practice that don't meet the above criteria (i.e., they are not based on a current dilemma facing the faculty and administration, avoid what's hard to talk about, or attempt in scattershot fashion to cover everything hosts have questions about) aren't as useful as they could be. Figure 5.1 presents some examples of problems of practice.

DEVELOPING THE PROBLEM OF PRACTICE

Where does the problem of practice come from? It is not a whim and does not emerge from thin air. It comes from data, dialogue, and current work. The problem of practice is grounded in some kind of evidence, preferably shareable evidence (in other words, not just the hosts' hunch, which is probably grounded in observation but is not in any form to share with the network). It's something the hosts are already working on or think they might need to work on. School and district improvement plans are often good resources for problems of practice, though sometimes those documents are more about compliance than about what the system is actually working on.

For example, at a school that was concerned about the learning of its special education population, the problem of practice flowed naturally out of related work.

FIGURE 5.1   EXAMPLES OF PROBLEMS OF PRACTICE

Our children often aren't getting opportunities to practice thinking, work with one another, or engage in problem solving through different types of modalities. As a result, our students are often unmotivated, unfocused, and off task. Lessons aren't consistently meeting the motivational and learning needs of students.

- What is the nature of the task?

_____

When trying to solve unfamiliar word problems, not all students apply what they're learning in math lessons. Teachers feel frustrated that the students don't use what the teachers have taught. Students don't make connections between the teachers' lessons and the task they are supposed to solve on their own. Teachers may not be checking for comprehension frequently or in meaningful ways during the lesson.

- How do teachers know what students know during the math lesson you see?
- What would students know and be able to do from the math lesson you see?

_____

Seventy percent of our students in special education did not pass the state test last year. In particular, they did not do well on the open-response questions in both math and English language arts. In many cases, they left those problems blank. We may not be providing these student with enough practice on open-response questions. We may be providing too much assistance so that when they have to tackle these prompts on their own, they do not know where to start.

- What kinds of tasks are students being asked to do in class?
- What are the different ways you see students begin assigned work in class?

The school shared with network members the following list of objectives the school had to prepared to make AYP (adequate yearly progress) in one year and to surpass AYP the next:

- To decrease the achievement gap between special education students and regular education students at our school.
- To have our special education students attain achievement levels as high as the state's special education students.

- To have all regular education students increase their level of performance on the state test by one level. To achieve this, we are focusing on two areas of weakness indicated by our analysis: math vocabulary (grades K–5) and number sense (grades 6–8).

The school then shared some questions it was asking and wanted the network to investigate:

- Are we, as adults, modeling the use of high-level math vocabulary related to our TERC/CMP (math curriculum) lessons so that students can be observed using it independently in their own speech?
- Overall, in any class, are *all* children involved in a high-level task? A high-level task can be defined as being (1) standards-based (using the science, TERC/CMP, or Literacy Collaborative curricula), (2) of high interest to the students, (3) hands-on whenever possible, (4) a task that pushes their thinking in some new way, and (5) a task that demands that they apply their knowledge. This question comes as a result of our achievement gap between regular and special education students. Special education students should be able to be observed doing the high-level tasks, but with accommodations to allow them to be successful.

The problem of practice emerges over several conversations at the host site and between the hosts and the facilitator:

- The hosts brainstorm some possible problems of practice.
- The facilitator helps the hosts hone those possibilities into a draft problem of practice that will be fruitful for both the hosts and the network.
- The hosts refine the draft, sometimes with more assistance from the facilitator, into final form.

The process is very iterative and may include other conversations and revision.

For the first step, hosts immediately run into the question of whom to involve in the brainstorming process and how to involve them. At a minimum, the host principal will be involved, and if it is a superintendents' network, the superintendent will also be involved. Beyond that, it's up to the hosts' discretion. Sometimes, the hosts will involve a few other people from a variety of roles, including central office personnel (e.g., deputy superintendent, head of professional development, head of a particular content area that the district is focusing on) and school-level staff (e.g., assistant principal, teacher leaders, instructional coaches). Some hosts use existing structures, like a school or district leadership team, to start the conversation about possible problems of practice, and others put together a group of teacher leaders particularly for the rounds visit. Some hosts have a broad conversation (e.g., whole-school faculty meeting), and others limit the conversation to a couple of people. We've seen a principal invite faculty members to brainstorm ideas for the problem of practice and write them on sticky notes. Then the principal took these sticky notes to an instructional leadership team meeting, where the team grouped similar ones together and chose one to focus on. We've also seen a superintendent and a principal meet and decide on the problem of practice on their own.

These choices depend heavily on context, and there is not one "right" approach. Nevertheless, it's critical to think about teachers' role in the process of articulating a problem of practice as they are the ones whose practice is being directly observed and who quite rightly will be wondering what to make of all these educators visiting their class. We've also found it easier and usually more meaningful to share the resulting data with faculty who have been involved in requesting it from the beginning.

However they do it, the participants emerge from the first step with a short list of possible problems of practice. Participants often find it helpful in this stage to see examples of problems of practice so that they get a sense of what rich problems look and sound like.

In the next step, a facilitator helps the hosts take the raw material of the brainstorm and shape it into a refined problem of practice. Some questions the facilitator might ask early on in the conversation include these:

- What are some of the strengths of your school? What areas need to be strengthened?
- How do you know about these strengths and weaknesses? What are your sources of data? How do you know whether you're making progress in these areas?
- What else have you been learning from these sources of data?
- What is puzzling to you about the data?
- What has felt challenging? What does your faculty continue to grapple with?

As the facilitator hears the hosts' ideas for the problem of practice, where those ideas come from, and the context of the host school or district, he or she is also reflecting back to the hosts what is being heard and offering language to capture their ideas: "What I hear you saying is . . . Is that right?" "It sounds as if we have several possibilities for a problem of practice: X, Y, Z . . . Which of those feels like one you want to dive into?" Often, the facilitator's role is to help narrow down the possibilities, which presents an opportunity to consider both host and network needs. Since one of the goals of rounds is to deepen the network's understanding, the facilitator is thinking about where the network is in its development. Sometimes, the hosts are thinking about this, too, but most hosts find it hard to think about their own needs and those of the network at the same time. It often works better for hosts to focus on their own work while the facilitator thinks about the interests of the wider network. The facilitator might steer the host more toward one idea if it's something the network has been discussing or would move the network to a deeper understanding of learning and teaching—it is still authentically a problem for the hosts and is one that will help the network. The problem of practice always comes from the hosts, not the facilitator.

For the final step in the process, it's helpful to have some time for the problem of practice to simmer. Does it meet the criteria of a rich problem of practice? Does it feel relevant and meaningful? Is it narrow and focused enough? Is it clear? Can plainer language replace any jargony words? Sometimes, the hosts will bring the problem of practice back to a wider faculty at this point. Once the hosts and facilitator are satisfied with the problem of practice, it's time to attend to other preparation for the visit (see exhibit A.4 in the appendix for information on some of the logistics required for a visit).

CHALLENGES TO DEVELOPING A PROBLEM OF PRACTICE

There are several common challenges that emerge when a network develops a problem of practice. Many of these challenges are simply issues of degree. For example, statements of the problem might be too detailed or too general; the hosts might provide too much or too little context for a problem; or networks might have insufficient skill or knowledge to adequately address a problem of practice. Let's take a look at some of the most common challenges.

Too Much Packed into the Problem of Practice

It's common for hosts to want the network to look at many things, in part because we all have several problems we care about at any given moment and it's hard to pick one. This is especially an issue early on for the network when everyone is learning how to do instructional rounds: The hosts will not yet see the value of focusing, and the network is not very skilled yet and thus will struggle to handle multidimensional problems and several questions for inquiry. After gaining some experience and skill, a network might be able to keep several questions in mind while in classrooms, but initially, it's helpful to have one question. What's the one problem that is at the root of the others, or that you most care about, or that you think is the most high-leverage? Even when the group is more experienced and skillful, it's hard to hold on to more than three questions or areas of focus while in classrooms. Early in our own rounds practice, we allowed hosts to name up to six questions, and we found ourselves having conversations that were less helpful for the school or the network—there was just too much to gather and discuss—and we ended up being shallow instead of deep.

Implementation/Audit Syndrome

Frequently, hosts want the network to look for evidence of something the hosts have been trying to implement, like literacy strategies or a new math curriculum. There is a fine line between using rounds as an audit of whether people are doing what they're supposed to be doing (not okay) and using rounds to find evidence that the instructional core looks as it should if the implementation were happening (okay). In other words, what would you expect to see in classrooms if the new math curriculum were being implemented well? One simple strategy for shifting the conversation is to focus on the kind of *learning* you want to see, as opposed to what kind of *teaching* you expect to see—in short, focus on students, not teachers. Sometimes, going back to the problem being addressed or the kind of learning you want to see can be helpful (e.g., students are engaged in too much procedural math and we want them to understand concepts, or we want students to be independent readers and writers). Similarly, grounding in data can help. Why are you interested in checking on this issue? What do you already know about it?

In one school we visited, the district had invested heavily in professional development around literacy strategies. It knew from self-reports and observations that teachers were doing the required number of strategies. The district thought that neither the teachers nor the students had internalized the strategies, so after conversation, it reframed what had initially been an implementation check to the following questions:

- What literacy strategies are students using?
- In what ways do teachers teach literacy strategies?

Note that rather than asking "Do you see . . . ?" questions that could be answered yes or no, they asked questions that were more open-ended and that prompted network members to collect evidence in those areas.

In another network, the host school had engaged in a year of professional development around "higher-order questions" (according to Bloom's taxonomy of educational objectives), and it wondered whether the network observers would see any evidence of those questions.[1] The school articulated its problem of practice: "Students aren't performing at high levels and teachers are primarily focused on recall and procedure." The focus questions were "What questions do you hear?" and "Who is asking or responding to them?" Note that the problem of practice doesn't ask for evidence of higher-order questions; it opens the focus a bit wider because the host school wanted to collect all the questions and then be able to examine them and see the distribution of what kinds of questions were being asked. In the debrief of the classroom observations, it quickly became clear that most of the questions were focused on recall and procedure, though there was more of a range of questions than when the school first started working on questions. This prompted a conversation both in the network and later at the school about the growth that was evident in practice as well as what the next level of work should be after considering the data.

Some of the implementation/audit tension is about framing and intent—are we going into classrooms to learn about the instructional core (interaction of teachers and students and content), or are we going into classrooms to check up on teachers? If the former, it's rounds. If the latter, it's not rounds. Implementation audits may have a place in your improvement strategy, but they're not rounds. Rounds are supposed to be about puzzles and shared inquiry and seeing every piece of data as a learning opportunity and as a guidepost on the Road to Support, not as thinly-disguised accountability. We don't do rounds to other people. We do rounds for ourselves and for our students. We do rounds together. If it feels like it's being done to someone, it needs tuning.

Too Broad or Vague Statement of Problem

The more specific the problem of practice is, the more specific and helpful the observational data and the recommendations in the next level of work will be. Vague problems of practice lead to vague observations and recommendations.

One host we worked with didn't want to focus her colleagues on a particular issue in her words, she didn't want to bias them and wanted their take on the whole picture. Thus, she gave them several questions that were variations on the three core questions we started with: What are teachers doing and saying? What are students doing and saying? What is the task? These are fine questions to use as a starting place, but they don't focus on any particular element of practice. As a result, the data and conversation produced are wide-ranging and a product of what each individual in the network values rather than what the host wants help with. The same network had wonderful, productive conversation in response to the above prompt about what questions they had heard and generic, unproductive conversation in response to these general questions.

It's not biasing the group to ask the participants to focus when they're in a class-room—the focus helps people be better observers. In fact, in this case, the host had particular problems of practice in mind (as we all do, even if they're implicit in our minds) and wanted to see if her colleagues would notice the same things without prompting. The feedback was too wide-ranging to serve as confirming or rejecting.

Hosts often want some verification of what they think they're seeing in their own system. The best way to check that is to be clear about what the problem of practice is and see what evidence your colleagues collect around it. A teachers union vice president underscored this idea when she explained what evidence meant to her: "I see it just as data. If you go back to the problem of practice that was generated by the teachers, you see what they want it [instruction] to look like. All we're doing is giving them the snapshot, and the learning is for them to take this and do something with it. We are careful to say—no value judgment—just say what it is. Just say what we saw."

Unlike other collegial conversations that may be biased by preconceptions, conversations during rounds are entirely evidence-based and therefore not as susceptible to individual agendas. If there isn't evidence, that will come out in the debrief.

Too Little or Too Much Context

Sometimes general questions can work if the context is specific. For example, "What is the task?" can be a rich question for a network, but it helps to know what some of the evidence around student learning looks like and what the system has been working on. With any problems of practice, it helps to have some context.

At a minimum, it's helpful to know some basic information, like how many students and teachers are in the host school and district, demographic information, and student performance highlights. Sometimes, the hosts also share information about special programs or features of the school or district (e.g., multigrade classrooms, inclusion of students with disabilities in regular education, Chinese language program, arts focus). The guiding principle is, What do network members need to know before they observe? Later on in the rounds process, the hosts may share more information, like what they have been doing to address this problem of practice. We find that network members are unlikely to read several pages of context, but are likely to read a one-pager, will pay attention to hosts giving the context aloud, and will refer back to any context write-ups (e.g., data charts) as they debrief and discuss the next level of work.

Network with Inadequate Knowledge or Skill for the Problem at Hand

If the problem of practice is something the network has not engaged before, the network must ask whether it needs any kind of knowledge, skill, or common understanding to address the problem of practice. If the answer is yes, the network must decide whether participants need it before they go into classrooms, or whether they can attend to it at another point, like after observations and debrief, but before the next level of work. We investigate this question more completely in chapter 7. When designing the problem of practice, the network must consider and plan for this question. If the problem requires more knowledge and skill building than the network has time for, then it might make sense to choose a different problem of practice. This is rarely the case in our experience, but sometimes, a more generic framing can shift a problem into something the network can engage.

OBSERVATION OF PRACTICE

The purpose of visiting classrooms is to gather data directly on the work of teaching and learning. This will be the raw material that participants use throughout the day's learning.

Often for rounds, there are no specific note-taking tools—just blank notepads. On other visits, schools may provide specific sheets for note-taking, depending on the problem of practice and the kind of evidence that the hosts would like to gather. They may want observers to keep tallies or to organize their notes in a way that will be most useful to the school after the visit. Some networks develop their own observation sheets to use across all visits.

Each rounds visit, before setting off into classrooms for rounds visits, we review our observation guidelines:

- Listen; don't interrupt the teacher or disrupt the lesson.
- It's fine to ask students questions as long as it seems appropriate at that point in the lesson.
- Talk with other network members during the debrief, *not* in classrooms or the hallway.

Networks make their own variations of these guidelines. While they are in classrooms, the goal of observation teams is to collect meaningful data without disrupting the learning. Talking with each other (even in a whisper!) in classrooms is disruptive and disrespectful, and we agree to hold off discussing what we've seen until the formal debrief after all the observations. Hallway talk tends to be evidence-light and judgment-heavy (e.g., "Wasn't that great!" "I'd be so bored if I were a student in there!").

Observation teams of four to six people then spread out across the school. (See sample observation schedule in table 5.2.) They file into classrooms and generally look for an unobtrusive place to stand as they orient themselves to the classroom. Some schools set up folding chairs at the back of the room; in other schools, network members slip into extra desks or lean against a filing cabinet. In either case, the position is only temporary, as observers will want to move around the classroom to see the work of a range of students and, when appropriate, to talk with students. In some schools, the teacher leaves extra copies of the current assignment in a stack for network members. In all schools, the teacher is encouraged to continue with his or her lesson as the visitors enter; no introductions or acknowledgments are needed.

One of the best ways to understand what's going on in the instructional core is to talk with students, which we highly recommend unless the teacher is directly instructing them. Some network members will feel very comfortable asking students questions, and others will need some help knowing what kinds of questions to ask. Brainstorming what to do when you're in classrooms, and in particular, what questions to ask students, is a good activity for the network to do together. Here are some of our favorite questions:

- What are you learning? What are you working on?
- What do you do if you don't know the answer or you're stuck?
- How will you know when you're finished?
- How will you know if what you've done is good quality?

TABLE 5.2 SAMPLE SCHEDULE OF A ROUNDS VISIT

	Group 1	Group 2	Group 3	Group 4
				Caz B.
	Carole L.	Joe D.	Larry B.	Russell C.
	Barbara V.	Candace D.	Mike A.	Robin H.
	Richard E.	Jack H.	Sarah F.	Chris S.
	Vinnie M.	Linda M.	Laura M.	Kathy W.
9:10–9:35	Rm A3, Gr. 1, Park	Rm E3, Gr. 6 Math/ Science, Attles	Rm A6, Gr. 3, Rodriguez	Rm C6, Gr. 5, Bennelli
9:35–10:00	Rm B7, Gr. K, Kleindorf	Rm A3, Gr. 1, Park	Rm E5, Gr. 6 Spanish, Costa	Rm E3, Gr. 6 Math/ Science, Attles
10:00–10:25	Rm E7, Gr. 7 SS, Lawrence	Rm A2, Gr. 2, Gomez	Rm A4, Gr. 3, McConnell	Rm E5, Gr. 6 Spanish, Costa
10:25–10:45	Rm A2, Gr. 2, Gomez	Rm E7, Gr. 7 SS, Lawrence	Rm E1, Gr. 6 Skill Building, Attles	Rm A4, Gr. 3, McConnell

	Group 5	Group 6	Group 7	Group 8
	Mary E.	Pat B.	Kate C.	Tim G.
	Joellen S.	Barbara B.	Liz C.	Maryann M.
	Joe P.	Damon S.	Paulette J.	Mary R.
	Carolyn T.	Debbie S.	Nancy M.	Ed Mc.
9:10–9:35	Rm E1, Gr. 6 Humanities, Heller	Rm E8, Gr. 7 ELA, Baker	Rm E6, Gr. 8 Math, Mozzer	Rm C5, Gr. 5, Jerumal
9:35–10:00	Rm E8, Gr. 7 ELA, Baker	Rm B6, Gr. K, Fellino	Rm C5, Gr. 5, Jerumal	Rm E6, Gr. 8 Math, Mozzer
10:00–10:25	Rm B7, Gr. K, Kleindorf	Rm D3, Ungraded, Watson	Rm C3, Gr. 4, Lawry	Rm C1, Gr. 4, Schiavone
10:25–10:45	Rm A1, Gr. 2, Hunter	Rm B7, Gr. K, Kleindorf	Rm C1, Gr. 4, Schiavone	Rm C3, Gr. 4, Lawry

We usually thank students for sharing their work and speaking with us at the end of an exchange. Student responses provide valuable data that observers write down to share with their colleagues later.

One dilemma that observers often face is whether to do any one-on-one instructing when they are conversing with students. While you're talking with students about what they're doing, you may notice that they are struggling with an assignment or are factually incorrect or are on to an interesting idea. You might feel that you could extend or redirect or lower their frustration level if you just put your teacher hat on and asked a question or pointed out something. Do you do it? Or does that skew your data or interfere with the teacher's turf? You are there as an observer, not as a teacher's helper, so now is not the time to be Super Teacher. Nevertheless, all of this work is to help students learn, so if the student you're talking with could use a little help as a learner and you have an idea about how to guide him or her (not do the work!), there is no rounds rule against it. We've done so ourselves many times. We are educators, after all. We just try to remember that we're there as observers and to save our superhero tendencies for when we're thinking about how to help the whole system help each of those learners.

■

Tips and Takeaways

Here are a few tips about the problem of practice and observing. Again, the point is that you are trying to improve learning in a network, not evaluate any educator.

- *Don't aim for the "perfect" problem of practice.* The network will get better at designing problems of practice over time, and the problem does not need to be perfect to be useful. If it meets the criteria of a rich problem of practice described earlier in the chapter, it will be helpful.

- *Look down, not up.* When observing in a classroom, focus on what students are actually doing, not what the teacher has asked them to do or what the conversation seems to be about. Remember the principles of the instructional core and the role of task and how it predicts performance. You have to see how students are engaging with the task to get a good picture of the instructional core.

■ *Focus on students, not the teacher.* When in classrooms, most educators' natural tendency is to focus on the teacher. Focusing on the teacher is a bit like watching the ball in a basketball or football game or watching the conductor in a symphony—a lot that's happening away from the ball or the front of the room matters for the result. Again, with the instructional core, you're interested in the interactions of teacher, student, and content, not just any one piece. You still want to collect evidence about the teacher, but in our experience, most people don't need to be reminded to do that. People do have to be reminded to focus on students. This is particularly challenging if teachers are doing most of the talking during an observation. However, the data on what students are doing in these classrooms while the teacher is talking could still be quite revealing.

CHAPTER 6

Doing Rounds Part 2:
Debriefing and the Next Level of Work

The principals in the network chatted quietly as they waited for the signal from the facilitators for the next step of rounds. They had just returned from visiting classrooms and, once all the teams returned to the library, would start the debrief. Since it was their third visit, there was less anxiety in the room about the steps of the process. However, there was a growing realization that signing up to participate in rounds was different from other professional development exercises. The participants didn't leave sessions with a folder full of answers. If anything, they often left with more questions. As one principal explained, "I came into this group feeling like I was a pretty good judge of teaching. But now I realize that I don't know as much as I thought. On that first day, as soon as people in my team started sharing their observations, I realized I was missing a lot. It's a humbling experience."

"When are they going to define good teaching for us?" asked Jonathan after the facilitators directed the groups to find their seats and begin sorting through their observations for specific pieces of evidence to write on sticky notes. "I don't have a problem doing these school visits and spending so much time observing. I just wish they'd be a bit more direct about what they think we should be seeing."

"Jonathan, I think you're missing the point," responded his colleague Marsha. "They want us to figure that out ourselves. We're supposed to use what we learn from our observations to come up with a definition we can all really share."

"And how are we supposed to do that?" Jonathan grumbled.

Even though Marsha was still learning to understand the steps herself, she sensed that rounds would help her be a better leader. At their last session, she'd gotten some real insights into questioning techniques that she was still mulling over. "I think it's about figuring out what leads to learning."

The final two steps of the rounds process are the debrief, in which the participants sift through and discuss the evidence they have gathered from classrooms, and the next level of work, in which participants take what they have learned from the debrief to recommend the next steps to make progress on the problem of practice. These steps can seem slow at first. It's worth being deliberate and thorough with these steps, however, since this is when the network participants start voicing what they know and believe, as well as what they are coming to understand and question about teaching and learning. Through the debrief and next level of work, network members start to build their collective understanding and their practice grounded in the instructional core.

OBSERVATION DEBRIEF

When the teams return to the library or another meeting space, they grab some coffee and try to refrain from talking about the classrooms visits until they sit down for a formal debrief of their observations. The conversation heads systematically up the ladder of inference as the group processes what it has observed. The purpose of the debrief is to consider the collected evidence together and to move from agreeing on what people saw to eventually agreeing on what learning would result from what they saw. There are three steps to the debrief: description, analysis, and prediction. Networks spend varying amounts of time on each step. They usually need to spend most of the time on description early in their rounds experience because they're still getting used to this skill and they're still calibrating their understanding of teaching and learning. All three steps are included in each rounds visit. Even experienced groups spend considerable time on the description since this is an important source of learning.

Description

Immediately after classroom observations, it always feels tempting, especially in the beginning, to jump to an analysis of the problem, to suggest a few actions the principal or teachers could take, or to otherwise engage in problem solving. This isn't the purpose of discussion at this point. This step of rounds redirects the lens of inquiry squarely back on to the data. It holds our gaze there when we are eager to move on. To do this, we deliberately debrief classroom visits through a process that requires participants to stay in the descriptive voice and to listen and learn from colleagues. First, people need time to reflect on what they saw and to select pieces of data—often called pieces of evidence—that are relevant to the problem of practice. Then, generally in small groups, the participants share what they selected. What qualifies as relevant is a concept that evolves over time as the group gets more consistent in both what it's looking for and what it understands to be important.

As a result of this uninterrupted and extended spotlight on classrooms, the members of a network learn to expand their vision to see more than what they normally see on their own. After debriefing her first observation with her team, one superintendent said, "I realized that all of my observations were about the teacher. Other people on my team noticed what the students were doing, and that made me realize that I hadn't paid attention to that." These discussions quickly reveal that being in the same room does not result in everyone seeing the same things. As the superintendent noted, an important first step in these conversations is to notice what you didn't notice.

Analysis

After coming to a common understanding of what the group saw, the next step of the debrief is to look at the evidence and begin to analyze the picture it presents. Making sense of the data together is a critical activity. The technique we most often use at this point is for observation teams to group the data in ways that are meaningful to them. With the data displayed in some way in front of them, the members of the group ask questions about the data and look for patterns. For example, one observation team noticed that across several classrooms, the teachers frequently asked questions that required single-word answers. ("A square has how many sides?" "The reason they saw the chameleon was because he turned bright ——?") The team wrote "questions with single-word answers" as a category and put several examples under the heading.

In addition to having the patterns emerge from the data, we sometimes find it helpful to use an external framework or pattern, like the revised Bloom's taxonomy or a set of content area standards. In one network that chose to use Bloom's, all the sticky notes clustered under the headings "remember" and "understand." While the conversation in both the description and the analysis is focused on the problem of practice, we allow space in the conversation to collect evidence that seems relevant/important, even if it's not something the hosts requested. Often, patterns that show up in the "relevant/important" category provide material for suggestions later on, during the next-level-of-work session. For example, during one debrief, an observation in the "relevant/important" category noted that desks were in rows facing the teacher. This prompted a discussion about how this might have decreased students' ability to talk to each other and potentially diminished the learning possible in that setting.

We've done the debrief in many different ways, and we continually adapt it according to what we think is working and not working. Here are some basic principles that are common to all of our debriefings:

- *Stick to evidence.* As we have discussed, during the debriefing, the conversation should only include evidence. Participants can help one another learn to restate judgmental statements in descriptive form. Prompts—like "What's the evidence that supports that idea?" or something more playful like "Just the facts, Ma'am!"—encourage colleagues to push each other when they hear someone slip into the normative language that masks specifics of practice. So, for example, when someone says of a teacher she's just observed, "She did a great job motivating the students," a colleague uses a previously introduced prompt to ask, "What did you see that makes you think that?"
- *Designate a facilitator/timekeeper.* Having someone keep an eye on time and move debriefing groups from one question to the next helps. We usually rotate this responsibility from visit to visit (using various strategies, like "the person whose birthday is closest to today is the facilitator/timekeeper," or volunteer, etc.).
- *Debrief by questions.* Sometimes we debrief by classroom (first talk about Room 101, then 102, etc.). Other times we debrief by the problem of practice focus question(s). This can help the group stay focused on the question (if there are multiple questions, we discuss question 1 across all classrooms and then question 2, etc.) and help see if there are any patterns across classrooms.
- *Debrief in small groups and then medium groups.* We usually debrief in small groups (the observation team of around four or five with whom we observed), and then in combined groups (groups of eight or ten, with two groups who saw some of the same classrooms at different times). Smaller networks may have a small-group followed by a whole-group structure.

- *Share talk time.* We often use a guideline like "everyone speaks once before any-one speaks twice" or "three before me" to help balance air time and hear from everyone.
- *Write things down to focus the conversation.* Sometimes we take notes in the small groups of four or five, which provides the host principal with detailed evidence for later if we didn't take notes on particular observation sheets. We consistently have the medium-size groups of eight to ten participants write something down on chart paper, usually three patterns of evidence.

Debriefing helps networks develop norms for what to look for in classrooms and how to talk about it, as described by one network member: "Groups often have different definitions of what rigor is. The activities and debriefings have caused me to reanalyze what I had thought of as good examples of rigor and high-level think-ing previously and have helped us come to a common understanding of what rigor means to our network."

SAMPLE DEBRIEF (DESCRIPTION AND ANALYSIS)

On your own (about ten minutes):

1. Read through your notes.
2. Put a star next to observations that seem relevant to the problem of practice.
3. Select five to ten pieces of data, and write each on an individual sticky note.

With your small group (about forty minutes):

4. Share observations of each classroom you visited. Help each other stay in the descriptive (not evaluative) voice.
   - "What did you see/hear that makes you think that?"
5. On chart paper, group the evidence in ways that make sense to you. Single pieces of evidence can be a "group." If a piece of evidence belongs in more than one group, copy it onto multiple sticky notes.

   Alternative
   - If you are using external standards (such as Bloom's taxonomy or NCTM math standards), as you discuss each classroom, use [Bloom's taxonomy] to sort your stickies. Add observations to the "relevant/important" category

continued on next page

SAMPLE DEBRIEF (*continued*)

on a separate chart. These are observations that don't fit on the [Bloom's] chart but are relevant to the problem of practice.

6. Label your groupings.
7. Identify patterns.

With your partner group (fifteen to twenty minutes):

8. Designate a facilitator (a taskmaster!).
9. Compare your charts, and identify patterns and contrasting elements.
10. Fill in a four-quadrant grid that summarizes the two charts that each of the small groups has when they get together.
    - Patterns
    - Contrasts
    - Evidence specific to the problem of practice
    - Questions

With the whole group (ten minutes):

11. Debrief what the groups have learned. What patterns did people see? What do people wonder?

**SAMPLE DEBRIEF (DESCRIPTION AND ANALYSIS)
FOR A MULTIPART PROBLEM OF PRACTICE**

On your own:

1. Read through your notes.
2. Put a star next to observations that seem relevant to the problem of practice. Try to pick at least one piece of evidence for each of the school's questions in its problem of practice.

With your small group:

3. Choose a facilitator/timekeeper.
4. Posted on the wall are three to five pieces of chart paper, each with different aspects of the problem of practice. Each small observation team spends a few minutes at each piece of paper discussing the evidence the team saw that pertains

to this question. Groups then move on to the next chart paper and add their evidence to the evidence that a previous group added.

Alternative

- Stay seated with your small group. Spend 5-10 minutes per question. For each question, each person shares a piece of evidence. Once everyone has shared a piece of evidence, go around again and share other evidence, or open up the conversation for a broader discussion of the evidence you saw related to that question. After you have addressed the questions, spend 3 more minutes discussing "Other"—are there other things you noticed that you want the host leaders to think about?

- In partner groups: Share your evidence and discuss what patterns you notice across the evidence. Spend 5 minutes on each question and 3 minutes on "Other." Concisely summarize 3 patterns you notice on chart paper and post your paper.

5. Help each other stay in the descriptive (not evaluative) voice ("What did you see/hear that makes you think that?").

6. Finish with a "relevant" category on a separate chart.

7. Afterward, do a "museum walk" to review the charts and identify patterns.

With the whole group:

8. Share patterns that the groups saw. What data did people notice in the "relevant" category?

Prediction

We've sometimes made the mistake of skipping prediction, assuming that we all see where the analysis is headed. In fact, it's the prediction step that often leads to collective *aha* moments and provokes important group learning. The goal of this step is to connect teaching and learning. Groups ask themselves, "If you were a student at this school and you did everything you were expected to do, what would you know and be able to do?" By linking the task and teacher's instruction directly to student learning, network members tackle the central question—what causes the learning we want to see? What specific teaching moves, what kinds of tasks, what forms of student engagement lead to powerful learning for students? This process ultimately helps identify potential areas for improvement and get clues into *how* these areas could be improved, including the specific moves that a teacher could use.

Sometimes, we ask the prediction question of the whole group for discussion. Sometimes, groups engage in a more formal process, initially writing up what students would know and be able to do in each classroom visited, and then gradually building their skill toward making predictions for the school overall rather than individual classrooms. Groups write these predictions on charts and then do a gallery walk and a whole-group debrief to see if the group is in general agreement.

The following is an example of the prediction step during one debrief session. An observation team discussed the following pieces of data: "Teacher referred to textbook and asked, 'What were the branches of government in ancient Greece?' 'What were the three social class groups in Greece?' 'What was the main resource?'" And from another class, "Class read story. Teacher: 'How many people did Clifford talk to in this story?. . . Who said that he would help him? . . . Who said that he was too busy?'" In response to the prediction question (If you were a student at this school and you did everything you were expected to do, what would you know and be able to do?), the group surfaced—and ultimately resolved—a fundamental difference of understanding that people hadn't known existed in the group. An experienced principal spoke first: "If I were a student in these classes, I would have solid reading comprehension skills—I would be able to understand what I read." This school leader was surprised to find that her colleagues disagreed. Up to that point, they had agreed on what they'd seen—they'd even sorted these same questions into a group that they'd labeled "information recall." Where they differed was in determining what the results of these student-teacher interactions would be. As they'd learned to do in the process, they returned to the classroom evidence to examine it closely.

The group eventually agreed that a student in these classes would know how to retrieve specific information from the text, would know how to listen for what a question is asking and respond, and would know how to read for factual information. By getting more specific, they also agreed that the evidence was not enough to determine whether students would be able to understand what they'd read. Perhaps if they'd stayed in the classroom longer, they would have collected evidence that would lead to that conclusion. However, from the interactions they'd seen, they could only be certain that students knew how to answer recall questions. By the end of the conversation, all the members agreed that this was not the same as reading comprehension. This realization was a new insight for the principal who had spoken first and who had equated recall questions with teaching reading comprehension.

At this point, people new to the process sometimes protest, "But we haven't seen the whole lesson. How can we draw conclusions about student learning just from this single slice?" And the questioner is absolutely right—we can't draw conclusions from a twenty-minute observation of one class, and we don't intend to. The goal of this conversation is not to evaluate the teaching we saw in that single classroom, but to understand the practice of teaching and the process of learning by investigating very specific interactions between the elements of the instructional core. Through this investigation, groups come to agreement about the nature of the learning that results from different interactions at the core. Finally, when we do this process across multiple classrooms and see patterns across classrooms, the data can be valuable to share with the host school and can provide a starting place for the later discussion about the next steps.

The prediction step highlights the importance of detailed descriptive data as a basis of all conversation. If the observations from this team had instead read, "The teacher asked questions about ancient Greece," and "Teacher asked questions about the reading book," the participants would not have been able to determine what students would know—it would have been harder to make the links between teaching and learning. Fine-grained description reveals the actual practices that result in—or do not result in—student learning.

Taken cumulatively, these debrief practices allow participants to describe the specific behaviors and structures they see that cause, enable, or at times diminish learning. This process sets up the final step of the rounds process, the next level of work.

THE NEXT LEVEL OF WORK

According to the principle of reciprocity, leaders who seek to improve practice are obligated to provide the resources and support teachers need to meet the improved standard.[1] During the next-level-of-work phase of rounds, network members think together about what these resources should be and what kinds of support will best meet the needs of teachers and administrators to move instruction to the next level. At this point in the process, it won't come as a surprise that the more specific and fine-grained the suggestions, the more helpful they are. Detailed suggestions that go beyond "form study groups" or "use faculty meetings" help the host school move forward concretely and force the rest of the network to practice linking administrative support to teacher action in the way they previously linked teacher moves to student learning.

This is the step—proposing solutions and recommending action—that many participants will have wanted to take from the beginning. Don't be surprised, however, if this is also the most difficult step to do well. Here again, people are used to speaking in broad brush strokes and using educational jargon (not to mention the "culture of nice" that adds to the indirectness, especially on anything that might be seen as critical feedback). When participants suggest "sharing exemplars" or "peer observation" as the next level of work, colleagues may nod their heads in recognition of these ideas—perhaps they've read about them in journals or tried them in their own schools. This apparent consensus belies the tremendous differences that exist in actual practice. It's likely that the variation in how school leaders envision these strategies matches the variation in how they imagine "effective questioning techniques" or other broadly defined teaching practices. For suggestions to be helpful, they need to be described at a level of specificity that links the recommended action to the stated problem of practice. Links between next-level-of-work suggestions and the instructional core need to be transparent.

We start with the assumption that teachers and administrators are already working their hardest with their best understanding of the goal in mind. It follows that in order for all involved players to make changes that will lead to improvement, they'll need to think and act—at least in part—in new ways. What will they need to learn to be able to do that? How will the system support this learning?

Before leaping into recommendations, it's helpful if the host principal or superintendent provides some additional context and the group takes another look at the morning's handout about the school and the district context: What are the current initiatives? What resources are available (e.g., math coaches, monthly principal meetings)? What has been done around this problem of practice already? What dilemmas do the hosts face? What questions are they thinking about?

At the school level, the handout might address these questions: Do the hosts have common planning time for teachers? How do they use faculty meetings? How many initiatives are new right now at the school? Do teachers have a formal means of communicating across grades? How many members of the faculty have received training in X (e.g., the new math curriculum or another new initiative)?

At the district level, information might address the following questions: What is the district's theory of action regarding professional development? How do principals learn about district curriculum and expectations? How often do principals meet to share ideas? What kind of professional development is offered to principals? Network members may have specific questions as well. The context helps the group make connections to what is in place, helps it avoid suggesting things that have been tried, and helps the hosts move to the next level. If the hosts don't present a perfect picture, but instead present what they're grappling with, the network can help.

After this context-setting step, the previous host facilitates the next-level-of-work part of rounds. With a peer's eye toward relevance and practicality, this colleague (or colleagues, in some places) ensures that the session determining the next level of work is meaningful to the current host. The previous host guides the network to generate a list of suggestions for the host school and district, combining the problem of practice, what they've seen, what they understand about adult learning, the history and context of the school, and what the school and the district have done in relationship to this issue. Following the suggestion of an early network member, groups often suggest what the school or district could do in the short and long term in three columns: "next week," "next month," and "by the end of the year." In some networks, groups create one three-column chart for district-level suggestions and another for school-level suggestions.

Again, learning occurs when group members push each other to get specific. When one group wrote "visit each others' classrooms," a fellow network member asked what the focus of the visits would be, how it would link to the problem of practice, if they would encompass multiple grade levels, and how people would keep track of what they'd learned. The host school won't use every idea generated, but the network members will surely benefit from coming up with the equivalent of effective lesson plans for school leaders.

While the focus is on improving teaching and learning in the classroom, the suggestions for the next level of work are not about "fixing" any one teacher or group of teachers. They are about developing clarity about good instructional practice and about the leadership and organizational practices needed to support the instruction at scale. Next-level-of-work suggestions are, if anything, more for administrators and other leaders (including teacher leaders) than for individual teachers.

While the next-level-of-work phase appears to most directly benefit the host school, it is a tremendous source of learning for the entire network—if it's done at a level of specificity and detail that requires real work from participants. Members question and probe the causal links their colleagues make. Take, for example, the case of a network that observed that teachers ask few open-ended questions and therefore students produced mostly single-word answers. Network members may hypothesize that if the faculty learns to ask open-ended questions and to ask more of them, the students will produce answers that are more thoughtful. This would lead a group to suggest that the school or district provide professional development or study groups focused on how to ask open-ended questions. However, a fellow network member might ask if it is enough for the teacher to simply ask more open-ended questions. Wouldn't students need to be taught how to answer questions that require a different level of thinking than the questions to which they are accustomed? In this case, the faculty would also need to learn how to teach new thinking skills to students, how to respond to incomplete answers, and how to provide feedback to support emerging skills.

Conversations like these teach district and school leaders the process necessary to unpack what's involved in supporting teachers to learn a new skill. Finally, suggestions for the next level of work for the host district or school may provide very practical solutions for visiting network members facing similar problems. One network member attested to this: "When we see what others are doing and what they need to do to get to the next level, it is often things we can also use at our own school."

In a network with district or school teams, having specific time at the end of a visit to sit, reflect, and make sense of implications is enormously powerful and generative. A simple prompt—"What did you learn from today's visit, and how does that affect your role and your practice back home?"—is enough to launch spirited discussions. In networks of single members (e.g., superintendents or principals or teachers), the question is still powerful, and the participants can write, reflect, and discuss with a neighbor. It can be tempting to skip this step at the end of the day, when it feels as if the group has already accomplished a great deal. Even reflection for just a few minutes is worth the time, however, as it allows people to apply what they've learned to their own context and to make internal commitments to practices they've discussed and come to value.

Networks develop their ways of concluding visits. Some networks post a "thank you" poster for teachers during lunch, and the network members sign it before they leave. One network does "warm fuzzies" in which the network members make positive statements at the end of the day—the network developed this practice early on in its work, when giving feedback felt harsh (the people giving feedback, not the hosts, struggled with this). The network members feel differently about feedback now, but they still like the warm fuzzies. In most networks, the hosts get the last word, which is a chance for them to thank their colleagues and reflect on the visit. Hosts are discouraged from "we tried this" or "that won't work here" responses, but instead are invited to try on the ideas for a while. They know they will have an opportunity to update the network in a month about the immediate follow-up.

WHAT HAPPENS NEXT?

The purpose of the visit is to support the learning of the network as well as provide feedback and suggestions for the hosts. The next step is for network members to apply what they've learned to their own context. At times, the facilitator might assign a task or "homework" assignment to ensure that this happens. After rounds focused on higher-order thinking skills in one district, network members went back into classrooms and observed with the same focus. They brought their evidence to the next session to share and categorize again as a way of solidifying the insights they'd gained about cognitive demand. In another network, participants took their collective definition of effective math instruction and visited classrooms to see how it held up. They came back to the following rounds session with suggestions for modifications based on what they felt was and wasn't captured in the group's current thinking. Another time, network participants committed to practicing their choice of protocol with a group before the next network meeting.

Most importantly, learning that occurs in the network changes people's individual practice as network members apply what they've learned in different ways. Below is a sampling of how network members have described how they apply what they learn in rounds to their own work.

A principal in Ohio reported that at her faculty meetings immediately after rounds sessions, she implemented the same professional development exercises she'd just experienced such as protocols for interacting with readings, activities to get familiar with Marzano's strategies or Bloom's taxonomy (see Further Reading in back of book). She laughed as she explained, "Now when I get back from rounds, the teachers all say to me, 'Okay, what did you learn this time?'" She explained with her usual courageous candor how the network influenced her own practice:

> It's made me look at what we do differently. Before [participating in rounds], I was looking at whether the kids were following the directions, listening to the teachers, well behaved. That's what engagement used to mean to me. After I started going to these sessions, and integrating Bloom's, we're looking differently at what teachers are

planning. We weren't looking at analyzing the task that we were asking them to do until after I started going through this process. When we started to talk more, we realized, it's not just about whether kids are on task; it's about kids talking to each other and about the tasks that we've given. Our kids aren't actively involved in what's going on—but then we realized that has a lot to do with how we plan it. . . . [When the network comes to our school] we want our problem of practice to be "Are kids collaborating and problem solving critically? Are teachers planning activities that allow for collaborating and problem solving around critical thinking skills?"

A deputy superintendent said that as a result of rounds, administrators think more specifically about what their role is in the next level of work: "The 'next level of work' has become a very common phrase now in our district conversation. We are all [at the central office] thinking more deeply about the supports—are the supports in place to help them make the transition? Rounds is helping give us that firsthand data and getting us to think more deeply about it, along with the time to think more deeply." This district also decided to thread a focus on task throughout all of its district professional development.

A teacher shared how his participation in rounds affected both his teaching and the work he did for the school as a teacher leader. Before participating in rounds, he'd thought of himself as a pretty good teacher. After a few rounds sessions, he said, "I realized I wasn't incorporating higher-order thinking into my lessons as much as I could." Furthermore, after the network visited his school, he reported that the visit changed the way he and fellow teachers developed their school improvement plan. "We'd been focused on how we would change percentage points on test scores, and we realized that we needed to focus on what *learning* we wanted to see—that's what it's all about."

In Cambridge, rounds became the way principals and central office staff collaboratively decided where to focus their work. The superintendent explained, "We learn more about our organization and our practices through rounds—it helps us see what we need to learn. If there's something of concern to us, we know that rounds will help us understand it better—it'll help us sort it out and decide on next steps. And when we use rounds, other things pop out at us as concerns that we know we need to deal with." The network participants had high expectations for rounds, as evidenced at the first principals' meeting at the beginning of their fourth year of using the model. The superintendent described the meeting: "At our principals' meeting last week, we developed an agenda for what the focus should be for rounds and our own next level of work this year. We came up with this long list, and we all laughed because it would take years to try to accomplish it all. But it didn't stop us." He joined the think-tank discussion the following week to narrow the list down for the network's consideration.

Many people ask, "But what happens at the host school after you leave?" Our primary means of supporting improvement at the host school is through the learning that school and district leaders do as members of the network. We expect them to learn—at every network meeting—how to support instructional improvement and how to bring their understanding of the instructional core to bear on their day-to-day practice. By sending them home with a clearer sense of the practices that improve teaching and learning, we expect them to make better decisions as leaders of schools and districts. However, on the day that they host, they also leave with an armload of data and suggestions specific to their district and school.

There is no single process for what happens next for the host in rounds networks. We've largely left this to the discretion of individual networks. Some principals take the data back to their faculty and lead discussions based on what people see. Others use the information to plan professional development for the following year. Some superintendents rethink their district's curriculum or realize they need to provide more specific professional development for principals to learn the new curriculum. Others discover that a districtwide discipline approach is stifling higher-order thinking, and they commit to reconsidering their approach. The amount of data that hosts receive is significant and it can help for them to have support in knowing what to do with it all.

In all networks, hosts report back to the group at the following session. They share what they learned, what they did as a consequence, and the next steps they're considering. Because of the schedule on rounds days, this sharing is usually one-sided, without much time for people to ask questions or give feedback. In Connecticut, superintendents wanted more. They developed a formal system of follow-up whereby superintendents visit each other as collegial thought-partners. Together, they brainstorm and solve problems regarding what surfaced in the visit, and together they share back with the rest of the network what they've planned and what the host has carried out. Another network resisted adopting this model for fear of the time commitment, but it agreed to check in with peers on a voluntary basis until it had enough experience to determine whether it was worth formalizing the system. In fact, colleagues were happy to volunteer to do follow-up. As this group demonstrated, the best follow-up is designed by the networks themselves. Asking network members what they expect of each other can build a powerful accountability system within the network.

■

Tips and Takeaways

The dialogue that occurs in the debriefing and next level of work is the heart of the network's learning. Here are a few tips to keep in mind:

- *Time always feels short.* No matter how long the debrief is, it always feels as though it's not long enough. Protocols, as described in this chapter, help people manage time efficiently and get to deep conversations more quickly. It also helps to remember that conversations are cumulative across the network's life. Over time, the debrief sessions start to feel more adequate as the participants' skills sharpen and the network develops common language and understanding.

- *Do all the steps of the process.* With time pressure and urgency for action, it can be tempting to skip steps. Resist the temptation. There's a reason for all of the steps before the next level of work. Instructional rounds proceeds from description to analysis to prediction to the next level of work. Staying in the descriptive voice, and avoiding the evaluative voice, is a central principle in the development of a strong common language of instructional practice. Analysis provides a way of creating common categories of discourse for understanding and communicating. Prediction provides a way of moving from the task as it is observed in classrooms to the likely student learning that will result. And the next level of work provides a way of giving useful advice grounded in actual classroom practice.

- *Link the description, analysis, prediction, and the next level of work.* Sometimes, the elements of the debrief can feel disconnected from each other and from the next level of work. Groups generate suggestions for the next level of work, and it's not clear how those suggestions are tied to the collected evidence. Documenting the conversation can help establish the through-line from description to the next level of work, which is especially helpful when the hosts do their follow-up work and converse with people who aren't part of the network and didn't hear how the network got to the next level of work. Our networks frequently use chart paper to document key parts of their conversation and sometimes make the connections explicit. For example, they might write down the observed patterns on one part of the paper and next-level-of-work suggestions on another.

■ *Talk about what follow-up happens outside the network.* However a network decides to address the question of what happens next, it's important to make this individual work public. Networks should include time for people to share how they're applying their learning outside rounds. People get good ideas from colleagues and receive an essential reminder that learning doesn't stop when they leave the host school. In many ways, that is when the real work begins.

CHAPTER 7

Facilitating Rounds

Cofacilitators Gary and Charlotte were busily crafting the plan for the next rounds visit. "How much do we need to do with the group to be ready for the problem of practice?" asked Gary. "I feel like the next levels of work all sound the same from visit to visit, no matter what the problem of practice is."

"I agree," said Charlotte, "but I don't think the group is ready for us to push on that yet. I think we need to back up and focus on description more. I think one of the reasons the next-level-of-work suggestions are not super insightful is that the descriptions are a pretty big grain size. Maybe we could take some of the evidence collected from the last visit and have people look at that and talk about what was helpful, what wasn't, and why."

"That's probably a good idea," said Gary, "but our time is so limited, and I really think we need to deepen people's knowledge about teaching and learning. We're using some language as if we all mean the same thing—rigor, engagement, higher-order thinking, checking for understanding. There's a lot of nodding when people say those words, but I'm not sure we all mean the same thing. Since the problem of practice this time is really focused on 'checking for understanding,' how about if we try to help people develop a picture of what it would look like for a teacher to be assessing whether students are understanding? Maybe we could show a video? Or is there a good article?"

"That makes sense to me," said Charlotte. "Let's do a quick description refresher in the morning before the observations, and then do some kind of professional development on checking for understanding before we talk about the next level of

work. I think we need to construct a list of what teachers and students would be doing and saying if 'checking for understanding' were happening."

"Okay," said Gary. "We just need to find a good video or text—and then cut something out of this agenda. It's too packed, as usual. What can we trim?"

G ary and Charlotte are engaging in the fun and challenging process of deliberately building the knowledge, skill, and shared understanding of individuals and the group—in other words, helping adults learn. While everyone in the network is responsible for helping each other learn, facilitators play a special role in nurturing, monitoring, and accelerating that learning.

Facilitators focus on content and process and move the network's work forward purposefully, while being responsive to the needs and opportunities that arise as the network develops. For facilitators who are new to rounds, even those with rich experience in helping adults learn, the process can seem somewhat mysterious or intimidating initially. It helps to remember the tenets of effective professional development, which rounds both embodies and reinforces: content-focused, sustained learning close to the work, context-specific with time for practitioners to apply what they're learning to their own settings.[1] It also helps to think about the role of the facilitator as essentially good teaching. You have to understand enough of the content: making clear causal links between teaching and learning, understanding the role of each element of the instructional core, understanding that we can't help students learn for the twenty-first century by doing the same things we've been doing to teach basic skills. You get to this content in rounds through effective teaching practices, like using time deliberately with clear learning goals, understanding that people learn by talking with each other and processing their learning in multiple ways, and helping people interact with text in meaningful ways, and so forth.

Nevertheless, facilitators are guides, not experts. They do not have to know everything. They do have to think like teachers. And they have to be learners. Effective rounds facilitators model the kind of learning they hope adults and children are doing in the school system. When their facilitation creates this kind of learning experience for the adults in the network, that will be one of the network participants' most powerful forms of learning. This chapter describes what it looks like to help adults learn in the rounds process. It offers suggestions for making rounds happen, listening and guiding, and cultivating the network.

MAKING ROUNDS HAPPEN

This section expands on the description of rounds to include some of the ways facilitators deliberately build the network's skill with each step of rounds as well as the network's understanding of learning, teaching, and the systemic leadership required to support learning and teaching. Facilitators maximize network learning through careful planning and targeted professional development.

Targeted Professional Development

Over time, many network members would come to deeply understand the rounds process and content simply through accumulated experience. However, most educators engage in rounds because they want to address student learning challenges now, not eventually, when the adults have accumulated enough experience. Fortunately, facilitators can accelerate the whole network's learning by deliberately building knowledge and skills as part of the group's experience.

The first place to focus is on the fundamentals of the rounds process: (1) problem of practice; (2) observation of practice; (3) observation debrief; (4) next level of work. With the problem of practice, the whole group benefits from an overview of what makes a good problem of practice, including some examples. Participants will use the examples as models, especially initially, so you want to choose examples carefully. The learning about problems of practice continues on a one-on-one basis as facilitators work with visit hosts to hone their problems of practice. The group deepens its understanding of problems of practice through regular reflection on how the rounds process is working, including the problem of practice. In one network we work with, this reflection led to a honing of the group's definition of a good problem of practice, including the distinction between checking for implementation and focusing on the learning you want to see in classrooms.

The combination of direct instruction, practice, and reflection works for the other elements of the rounds process as well. For the observation phase, many people aren't sure how to take notes or discover that their method for taking notes isn't as helpful as they'd like when they get to the debrief. One technique that demystifies the process is to have facilitators and network members share their notes. If you do this while watching a video (e.g., as people are learning to see in the early stages of rounds), everyone has a common reference point from observing the same classroom.

We've had success with two facilitators taking notes on transparencies and then sharing the notes on an overhead projector (e.g., "This is how I get oriented to a room. I notice . . . Then I started to really focus on the problem of practice . . . I didn't quite capture everything the teacher said, but I tried to note pretty accurately what the students were saying. Here is where I just couldn't keep up, so I put ellipses to show that there was more happening there. Down here, I went back up and filled in some of my notes. I noticed I was focusing on the teacher a lot, so I scanned the room to see what students were doing while the teacher talked. . . ."). Seeing more than one example is helpful for showing that there is more than one "right" way. After seeing how we record some things in great detail, the participants are often sharper in their own note-taking, which later helps when we're debriefing. You can do a similar kind of "show and tell" or "think aloud" later in the rounds process, in which you have participants share, compare, and discuss their note-taking. If people share in the same small group with which they were observing, they will all have taken notes on the same classes.

Notes provide the raw material for the debrief. Thus, important questions to consider are: What kinds of evidence further the group's learning? What kinds are less helpful? There are several ways to consider these questions, from a brief conversation to more formal methods such as examining samples of past descriptive evidence from the network or coming up with a rubric to guide people in the kinds of evidence to collect and share. For the next level of work, ask the participants what skills a teacher, principal, or superintendent would need to support the kind of learning you're focused on for a particular visit. This prepares people to think more specifically about next steps the host school or district should take.

There is more to rounds than just moving through the problem of practice, observation, debrief, and next level of work. Facilitators also help networks deepen their understanding of particular aspects of teaching and learning related to the problem of practice. A goal of rounds is that the participants will come to a shared understanding of teaching and learning. To do this, some networks have focused discussions around very specific aspects of practice before and after classroom observations. This allows people to capture more relevant data during observations and deepens the conversation about actual practice since people have a shared understanding of what they hope to see.

For example, after visiting classrooms at a school that asked the network to focus on teachers' questioning skills, the network members read sample teacher questions and grouped them according to cognitive demand. This prepared people to analyze what they'd seen in classrooms that morning. A network focusing on higher-order thinking looked at transcripts of teacher-student interactions to identify the types of interactions that promoted the greatest cognitive growth for the student.

Reading and discussing relevant articles can be a useful introduction to a school's problem of practice. Members of one host district shared an article that had been the focus of district discussions about academic rigor. This allowed the network to begin to define rigor and then analyze the subsequent classroom data according to this definition. Sometimes, the facilitators identify relevant reading and use a text-based protocol to structure the group's conversation (see Further Reading for some suggestions about where to find protocols). Common texts help networks develop a common language and understanding of learning and teaching.

Networks structure this targeted professional development in different ways, in part according to the available time for the network's meeting and in part according to when the professional development seems most useful. Some networks integrate the professional development into the visit day. For example, networks might designate approximately an hour before visiting classrooms and an hour at some point during the debrief session to focus on a specific aspect of practice. Sometimes, the pragmatics of the schedule don't allow much time in the morning before classroom observations and the group is limited to some time later in the day. Some networks go through a rounds cycle at one school and then devote time at the end of the day to prepare for the next visit. This can be hard because people are tired at the end of a rounds day and not as receptive to learning, but it has the advantage of allowing time for the participants to digest new learning before applying it. Of course, this approach also means that facilitators must have already worked with the next host to identify the problem of practice and already designed the professional development to accompany the problem of practice, which requires planning ahead.

Other networks build in additional sessions to meet the need for professional development. On the day of the school visit, these groups cycle through the four components of the rounds process. The group then reconvenes at a later date to delve deeper into what people saw and connect it to larger issues of teaching, learning, and their own leadership practices. The time and frequency of reconvening varies (see chapter 3 for a summary of our current networks' meetings). Networks make choices about professional development in light of existing convening structures, the distance participants travel, the time participants are willing to commit, and the group's sense of what time it needs for learning.

In any of these cases, there is always much more to learn and discuss than time in which to learn and discuss it. Part of the facilitators' task is to home in on what critical piece of learning will advance the network's knowledge and skill and to then design the learning experience within a limited time frame. Often this means choosing *one* article, exercise, or experience rather than the four you think the group really needs. Keep in mind that the network's learning, like all effective professional development, continues over time. There may only be two hours this month, but there is next month and the one after, too. As with all professional development, the quality matters more than the quantity.

Careful Planning

The deliberate scaffolding of knowledge and skill during rounds involves strategic planning. Good planning requires adequate time, collegial input and collaboration, and careful attention to the resources of the group and how to manage them.

We generally devote one and a half to three hours of preparation time for every hour of face-to-face time that we have. Planning may include looking for relevant literature and planning how the group will interact with the text in a meaningful way. It may include designing an activity that requires leaders to construct a model or rubric for learning or leadership. It also includes time to meet with school and district leaders to determine the problem of practice, as well as time to design the debrief and follow up on logistical considerations like the visit schedule with the host school.

Facilitating rounds involves considerable learning for the facilitator. Working with colleagues is a critical means of increasing this learning. One of the reasons we strongly encourage networks to have cofacilitators is so that the facilitators together have the opportunity to brainstorm lesson plans, to diagnose why a network may feel stuck, to assess what the group needs to revisit, and to identify struggling learners and what supports they need to refocus their learning. Colleagues bring another perspective on what the group needs and help raise your awareness of your own biases (e.g., perhaps you're focusing more on process than content, favoring question askers over silent types, or missing opportunities to push the group's learning). If you do not have a cofacilitator, we highly recommend engaging a thought partner to run ideas by.

In addition to a cofacilitator, networks of facilitators can be a powerful source of support and learning. For example, the Iowa Leadership Academy Superintendents' Network is developing a separate network just for facilitators. Facilitators meet monthly to share ideas, questions, challenges, and strategies from their networks. They use videoconferencing to connect with a more experienced rounds facilitator (in this case, one of us) for an hour during those meetings. Technology can support facilitator networks in other ways, like having a Web site that is populated initially with some support documents (e.g., see "How to Schedule a Round Visit: Example of Notes for a Host School" in the appendix). Facilitators can then use the site as a living virtual library that houses materials they develop as well as the myriad options available with online technology, such as engaging in discussions or doing a "webinar" about a particular piece of learning with which facilitators need support. The network facilitators in Ohio use a similar system, which they call their "pantry" because it stocks useful ingredients for the facilitators to use when they are putting together their lessons.

Facilitator collaborations can be smaller and more informal as well. The four of us have met monthly to share our learning across multiple networks. These conversations continue to generate more questions than answers and "feed" our work in nutritious ways. Gradually, we decided to share our learning and our challenges with a wider audience, both at conferences and in writing. We've found that preparing for these public presentations has helped us learn more about our individual and collective beliefs and assumptions and has pushed our own practice. We highly encourage you to engage with your colleagues in some public sharing of your work. Writing in particular forces a kind of clarity beyond a conference presentation.

Another dimension of planning is thinking strategically about network resources, in particular time, energy, and grouping. A key resource at your disposal is time, and you have to manage it carefully. How do you optimize learning? Not by packing in as much as possible or by making a ten-hour workday. We've made these mistakes, and the glazed-over looks on participants' faces as well as their feedback have convinced us to avoid making them again. Questions that help us trim down our goals include the following:

- What do we really want the participants to understand at the end of this session? Even though we know better, we sometimes get caught up in activities and lose sight of purpose.
- What is most essential for the participants' learning? What activity or activities could we cut? A good rule of thumb for us is to cut at least one activity that we have planned in a day. We always overplan.

- How are all the activities connected? Are they tightly linked? Is there an opportunity for depth over breadth? In our desire to address a number of topics that seem essential now, we sometimes spend too little time on two or three topics or activities rather than devoting all the available time to a single topic. It always works better when we go deeper.

Another critical resource is the network participants' energy, both mental and physical. Instructional rounds is draining work. People can only absorb so much at a time. Attending to group interaction ensures that you keep people mentally alert and able to contribute to the process. We like Bob Garmston's metaphor for finding the balance of process and content: chewing gum.[2] He thinks of gum as the content and chewing as the process. Too much gum without time to chew is uncomfortable and frustrating, and too much chewing with little gum is unsatisfying as well. Times for people to turn and talk with a table mate provide opportunities to "chew" on thought-provoking questions and help people hold on to what they're learning. Processing time also rejuvenates the mental energy of the group. The change in the room is noticeable when people have been listening for a while (either to the facilitator or to colleagues sharing during a whole group discussion) and then they are given a reflective question to talk about with a partner. First, there's a bit of tentative talk, which—with a compelling prompt—grows until the room is full of energy as people lean in to each other, nod their heads, move their hands, laugh. It's as if you poured energy into the room. It's as if, after all that breathing in of listening, you've finally given them time to exhale through processing with others.

Physical energy matters, too. People can't passively listen for hours at a time. Or rather, they can, but they don't do it very well, and it usually doesn't result in much learning. Sleepy afternoons are a good time to have people stand up and create wall charts, walk across the room to reflect with a partner on what they've just heard, or do a gallery walk of other groups' charts. We use sticky notes a lot, in part because they invite people to reach across a table to physically move ideas around. On one beautiful sunny afternoon, we sent partners outside for a fifteen-minute "walk and talk" about an article on program evaluation. They came back to the group refreshed and ready to debate the merits and limitations of the content. There is always a content purpose to these activities, but we try to be mindful of incorporating movement and managing physical energy. Breaks are important, too, and help participants get more learning out of the time they're "on." We try to take a break (a short break or lunch) every ninety minutes, and definitely don't go more than two hours without a break. If we go too long, the participants let us know by getting fidgety, glazing over, or slipping out of the room. When we see that, it's time to take a break, even if we didn't plan one.

The people in the network are a resource, and the way you group them is another strategy to manage to maximize learning. We think a lot about grouping when planning and usually have a variety of groupings during a rounds day, particularly for the professional development time. Considerations for grouping include when to be random and when not; how big to make the groups; when the whole group needs to talk and when it does not; and how to share ideas in the whole group. We want everyone in the network to talk with everyone else, and thus we sometimes do random groupings or mix groupings from one session or part of a day to another. When we do random groupings, we do them as efficiently and transparently as possible. If the participants can see that the groups are random, they're less likely to waste time and energy trying to figure out why they're with particular people or wishing they were with other people. Here are a few ways to randomly group efficiently and transparently:

- Count off up to the number of desired groups.
- Have participants choose a colored pipe cleaner, piece of paper, or popsicle stick with a group number on it.
- Have participants take a sticker when they walk in, and have the number of different stickers equal to the number of desired groups (e.g., flowers, cars, fish, and shoes)—this one's a little silly, but silly isn't necessarily a bad thing.

Sometimes it makes sense to group the participants by a common characteristic (e.g., role in a cross-role network, elementary or secondary school level in a principals' network, size of school or district). Sometimes it makes sense to design the groups by expertise and personalities. We pay attention to gender, race, ethnicity, and experience when grouping as well—our goal is not always to distribute these characteristics evenly across groups, but we do try to be mindful of them because they can matter for participants' learning. Why we choose one strategy over another depends on context and purpose; the key is to be purposeful.

We tend to use four- or five-person groups a lot because they're big enough for a range of ideas and small enough for everyone to have time to talk. When it makes sense for the entire network to have a conversation depends in part on how big your group is. The bigger the network, the more we tend to maximize small group time and minimize whole-group time. In smaller networks (e.g., of about twelve people), we often have more whole-group time because there is opportunity for dialogue and multiple voices. However, we still use lots of small-group time even in smaller networks because that is where participants often have enough time and safety to hash out the details of language and understanding. Many people are more willing to share in a small group than in a large one.

Of course, small groups are only learning spaces if they function well. It's important to build accountability and support into group work. Directing people to chart their work generally makes the groups more focused on the task. Assigning group roles such as timekeeper and facilitator helps keep things moving along in groups. We tend to assign roles randomly, to give different people the opportunity and responsibility for these tasks over time.

Another key to using small groups is having ways to share the small-group conversations with the whole group. You want the depth that comes from small groups and the shared understanding that comes from whole-group conversation. Some ways to go from small group to whole group include chart paper, gallery walks, and specific directions and interventions when sharing. It's hard to listen to multiple reports; directions like "only share what's new" or having a one-minute time limit help participants share the essentials.

LISTENING AND GUIDING

As stated earlier in this chapter, facilitating the network means thinking like a teacher and being a learner. Facilitators listen continuously to the members of the group to learn what the group *wants* to learn. At the same time, facilitators think continuously about what the group *needs* to learn and what will help with that process. They listen and guide by soliciting input and feedback, moving forward with a coherent agenda, and differentiating.

The best resource in any learning situation is the learners themselves, so it's important to create multiple ways for network participants to give you input about what they want to learn as well as feedback about what they've learned and how the process could have been improved. Good facilitators are always collecting feedback and input from the group—sometimes informally through noting people's responses to different protocols and prompts, other times through formal systems of input. There are several ways of soliciting this information from learners during rounds:

- *Plus/delta chart.* At the end of each session, draw a two-column chart. On the left-hand side, write a plus sign. On the right-hand side, draw a small triangle, a delta, which is the symbol for change. Frame the reflection questions as "What's helping you learn? What worked well for you today?" and "What could help you learn more? How could the learning be improved?" When you ask for feedback like this, it's important to communicate that you genuinely welcome information about what didn't work. Sometimes a group will feel that it can show its appreciation for a facilitator by saying there's nothing that could be improved. This deprives the facilitator of important learning and the chance to increase participant learning. We often encourage groups by saying, "We really love deltas. Please give us some deltas." One way to communicate openness to feedback is to ask for clarification rather than to get defensive. In fact, we generally try not to comment at all while recording plus/deltas. The best way to let the group know that suggestions for improvement are welcome is to act on them as quickly as possible. Sometimes we bring out the plus/delta chart from the previous meeting and talk about how today's agenda builds on the pluses and addresses the deltas, including being honest when today's agenda doesn't exactly do either of those things. It's amazing how quickly a group's learning will improve if you spend five minutes each session doing a plus/delta. If you're really pressed for time or want a broader range of anonymous answers, participants can write their plus/deltas on sticky notes and post them on the chart on their way out.

- *Think tank.* In our most recent work with networks, we've found it helpful to ask for a small group of volunteers to meet in between sessions to partner with the facilitators in reflecting on previous sessions and planning upcoming ones. Think-tank members should be representative of the group (i.e., serve in multiple roles if the network is a cross-role network), which may require a little proactive recruitment. Meeting in person produces a more personal dynamic, but phone conferences work well, too. While the facilitators still plan the nitty-gritty of the sessions, the think tank provides invaluable input on the big picture and helps ensure that the network is meaningful for participants. Think-tank members also become more knowledgeable about rounds by participating in the planning and often play important leadership roles in the whole group, helping shift responsibility for the group's learning to the network rather than the facilitators.

- *Surveys.* Online surveys are easy to assemble (see SurveyMonkey.com or Zoomerang.com, for example) and can provide a quick dip-stick assessment of any aspect of the network—what people want to learn more about, how people want to learn it, when people want to meet, and so on.

- *"Parking lot."* Posting chart paper as a "parking lot" for questions and comments gives participants an informal way to communicate when they're thinking about something and gives a place for the network to hold questions that emerge in discussion but may not be appropriate to explore further right now. The network then looks at the parking lot periodically to see if the contents have been addressed or need further dialogue.

- *Individual follow-up.* Following up with individual network members is a crucial way of getting input and feedback on what is working and what isn't. People who are silent, struggling with the rounds practice, frustrated, or skeptical are rich sources of useful information. Understanding their thinking helps the facilitator clarify misunderstandings and misconceptions or adjust the framing of a particular part of the process. Seek these people out at breaks and lunchtime! Engaging in an unfamiliar process like rounds is often disorienting, and facilitators can build trust through careful listening and responding to people's concerns. You won't be able to remove the disequilibrium that comes from learning the process, but you can remove distractions that prevent some people from tackling the real work.

With visits to different schools each time you meet and with network members often from different districts, there's a real risk that rounds sessions will feel disconnected and unrelated to people's individual work contexts. To avoid these pitfalls, facilitators carefully balance the needs of the host school with the needs of the network and look for ways to thread continuous learning from session to session. This is the leadership dance of getting ideas from the group and simultaneously steering the group. Facilitators authentically take direction from the group and make the pieces fit together coherently by looking for themes and making the group's learning visible.

A common focus for visits helps tremendously with coherence. The focus must be in an area where every participant feels he or she has challenges (i.e., problems of practice) that, if addressed, would improve student learning. If that criterion is met, the participants will stay involved and learn, even if the focus isn't their top choice. If that criterion isn't met, the network isn't serving all its members and participants may lose interest. A facilitator can help participants choose a focus by suggesting the notion of a common focus and its potential for encouraging depth and progress. He or she can nudge people to select the first few problems of practice of the network with similar themes and can point out some of the challenges that are common across the network. If people resist choosing a focus, let it go. Participants may need to experience the network for a year before they see the potential benefit of a common focus. In our networks, participants have sometimes chosen the focus explicitly; other times, the focus has emerged as a common interest over several rounds visits. The foci are usually at a variety of grain sizes, and networks tend to refine them with more specificity as they dive deeper into the topic. Examples of foci are higher-order thinking, math, how teams work at all levels of a district, and twenty-first-century skills.

With any topic, the use of external texts and frameworks contributes to a coherent agenda that builds from one session to another. As already noted, external texts and frameworks (e.g., someone else's definition of twenty-first-century skills, or NCTM's math standards) provide a common reference point. They also show that it's not just whatever the group thinks; other people have done some thinking about this topic, too, and sometimes that thinking raises the group's own standards or shapes the group's understanding of a topic. Despite all this, external texts and frameworks are useful insofar as they help the group develop its own shared understanding in a particular area. Their purpose is not to provide "an answer" or short-cut the group's effort to make sense of the topic. The network still has to negotiate its own vision of learning, teaching, and leadership.

Facilitators need to help make connections as well as keep reminding the group about the network's purpose. In other words, facilitators help the network keep both the forest and the trees in view at all times. Most participants will focus on the trees and may not see the forest unless someone points it out to them. Documenting learning provides multiple opportunities for connections and forest views. Rounds sessions generally result in many sheets of chart paper filled with group thinking. These charts help remind the group of previous sessions' discussions and agreements. We've seen networks keep working drafts of "powerful teaching and learning" in their focus area and continue to refine the drafts over time. Reflecting work back to the group ("Here is what we were working on last month," "Here are some examples of description that you wrote a year ago. How has your data collection and sharing changed?") creates a through-line between network sessions and makes the group's learning visible.[3] Stepping back and looking at their own work as data helps the group members see how much they have learned and identify areas for potential growth.

Documenting learning also provides rich clues about the group's understanding that facilitators can draw on in planning. For example, charts with sorted observation data give a good assessment of both whether the group understands how to be descriptive and how people think about teaching and learning. Reading next-level-of-work suggestions gives an idea of what the group understands about leadership and whether it's connecting ideas directly to the district context or if it needs more explicit instruction in how to do that.

CULTIVATING THE NETWORK

Being a learner involves taking risks. One network participant reflected to the group, "It feels safe to be a learner in here." Facilitators help create the conditions under which learning occurs by building trust within the group, developing lateral accountability among network members, and transferring responsibility to the group.

The research on trust reinforces what we know from practice: Trust matters a lot for learning and performance (see chapter 8 for more on trust).[4] Trust takes time, and there are several things facilitators can do to accelerate and nurture its development. First, use protocols to provide safe spaces for people to learn. One of our favorites early in a network's development is a *Hopes and Fears* protocol, in which you ask participants to describe their hopes and fears for instructional rounds.[5] Protocols range from formal methods for discussing texts to informal guidelines for managing talk turns. Next, help people get to know each other, including elements of who they are outside the educational environment. Icebreakers may seem like a waste of time, but they help people get to know each other as people and can encourage risk taking by building the risk gradually. For example, the participants could answer prompts like these:

- "What's something you're proud of?"
- "What's something you're looking forward to?"
- "Tell someone something non-education-related about yourself that other people are unlikely to know."
- "Tell someone about something you'd like to learn."
- "Tell someone about what your fashion style was in middle school."
- "Tell someone what part of rounds feels least comfortable to you."

Safe risk taking is both a product and a producer of trust. One way to encourage risk taking is to model it yourself. Be transparent about your own learning: "I'm really working on not overpacking the agenda. . . . I struggle to stay in the descriptive mode. Sometimes I just want to stand on a chair and tell you what I really think. . . . I'm a learner here, too. I feel as though I'm understanding more deeply why it matters to have a theory of action. I didn't get that as much before—even when we were drafting our theories of action."

Another way to encourage risk taking is to publicly notice and celebrate when people take risks: "Linda, I heard you disagree with Justin. That can feel really risky. What helped you do it? It might have been easier to just go along with the conversation and nod your head. That precedent will help people speak honestly in here." After answering a question, you might note, "Collette just asked a question. That will help everyone's learning!" Or after a debrief session: "Raise your hand if you disagreed with something someone said during that debrief. Now raise your hand if you disagreed *and* you said something about it out loud. Look around—these folks are helping to create an honest and open environment for all of us." You can also encourage the group to adopt risk taking as a goal and then reflect on how it did with that goal at the end of a session. Following up with individuals to acknowledge their risk taking or to encourage them to do so helps, too.

Another way to build trust is to provide social time. Our networks often have mingle time over coffee and a light breakfast at the beginning of a rounds day. We used to think this was enough social time and had thirty-minute lunches, often working lunches. We took the same approach to breaks, initially keeping them to five to seven minutes. We were planning the minimum amount of time needed for the break so that we would have more time for learning. Through the feedback process, participants told us that they needed longer breaks, including lunch, and they didn't want to work during lunch. This was not because they were lazy. In fact, most of them typically didn't eat lunch every day and went hours without making it to the restroom. What they realized faster than we did was that the breaks were critical times for them to catch up with each other and talk about everything from work challenges to vacation plans. A lot of the trust and relationship building in the group happens in these informal times, and it's important to create enough space in the schedule so that this kind of talk can happen. In another network, we've had to enforce the social time—some participants would rather work all day, while others would rather work through the break and go home earlier. We simply tell people that they'll learn better if they take breaks and that the informal time matters for the group.

Finally, a great way to build bridges with colleagues is to laugh together. As with other trust-building activities, laughter is sometimes tied to content and sometimes not. In either case, it can be quite quick, and it's not a waste of time. For example, we have people sing "My Bonnie Lies Over the Ocean" and change positions (either standing or sitting) every time they sing a word that starts with *b*. And we poke fun at ourselves a lot—we find that we never run out of material. In addition to the collegial spirit laughter generates, it also helps to create relaxed alertness, which is the optimal state for learning. After one such activity, a participant reflected, "I remembered today that it's okay to have fun. We work so hard all the time that we forget to have fun. This work is fun, too, and we need to remember that. I'm going to try to incorporate more fun with my teachers."

The second component of cultivating the network is developing a sense of *lateral accountability*—in other words, network participants take on the task of holding each other to agreements and nudging each other. This does not happen naturally in a group without the facilitators' encouragement. A critical initial key step is to establish group norms and refer to them. Norms aren't symbolic; they are a living document that guides group behavior and expectations. But this can only be true if you explicitly work with them. One way to work with norms is to check in frequently with the network members about which norm they want to work on today, which they felt the group did well, which they saw in action, and so on. In one network, we made table tents of the norms so that everyone could refer to them easily. In all cases, we ensure that the norms are visible during every session and we refer to them. We have also occasionally had members of the network serve in a process monitoring role in which they give the group feedback about how well the group was sticking to its norms.

Another way to work with the norms is to periodically ask the group to revisit and revise them. We saw a marked decrease in the use of cell phones after we asked one network's participants what they wanted the norm to be regarding cell phone use. After a particularly challenging session, one network decided to add a norm mandating descriptive language during rounds. At the end of its first year, one network refined its long list of norms to a handful that they could remember. During a norm check-in at the beginning of its second year, another network adjusted its "buy in or bow out" norm to make it clear that the group was committed to engaging in the four elements of instructional rounds but also wanted to encourage critical feedback to improve the process. The conversation about this norm evoked a new feeling of ownership within the group. After publicly encouraging more active engagement, the group focused on the work with increased vigor and enthusiasm.

Facilitators new to instructional rounds have asked if they can save time by borrowing a set of norms from another group. While these norms could guide their work, the network would lose the sense of personal accountability that comes when norms are created *by* the group *for* the group. Norms are requests that specific colleagues have made of each other—behaviors that they have said would help them learn. Here are some examples: Be honest; share when you don't agree; listen reflectively; check that you understand; support the work of the team when we're together and in between meetings (be present, give time for the work, provide resources); focus on practice and evidence; celebrate success; trust, respect, and honesty replace the "culture of nice"; be present and participate. Norms serve as a foundation for lateral accountability because they are one articulation of the network's commitments to each other. Once articulated, norms are something that participants can help each other with and hold each other to.

Another dimension of lateral accountability is network peers holding each other responsible for taking action through their participation in the network. For example, the host of the previous visit could share what has happened since the last visit or prior hosts and some people who have not been visited recently could share a report of their work. This ups the ante quite a bit and is even more outside most participants' collegial experiences than is holding each other to norms or to sticking to description in the initial part of the debrief. Part of having a professional practice is holding each other accountable for the practice, which in the case of rounds includes follow-up action. The network decides what this accountability looks like. Be prepared to push the importance of it early and often and to provide some ideas about what it could look like. Accountability for action works best as accountability and support, whether informal or formal.

At first, most network participants want facilitators to be the enforcers, problem solvers, and answer bearers. Our strategy is to put these responsibilities and opportunities back to the group, while supporting the network in responding to them. One of the main goals of putting things back to the group is what we call *transfer of agency*. Transfer of agency is institutionalized starting at the second visit. At this point, the network participants begin formally leading the work. The hosts from the previous visit facilitate the next level of work. They shepherd the group through this phase of rounds and ensure that the current host is well served. At the third visit, the second hosts facilitate the next level of work, and so on.

The idea is that the responsibility for the group moves from the facilitators to the group. The time to start giving the group responsibility is usually earlier than you think. The ultimate goal of the leadership dance referred to earlier is that the group direct more and more of its own learning. Over time, we would expect the facilitator's role to shift from teaching the rounds process to being a "critical friend" in noting what the group has learned, honing in on points of struggle, reflecting on ways to surface these tensions, providing external sources that are relevant to the group's learning, and using protocols or lesson plans to help the group interact with the resources effectively. The group doesn't have time to do all the planning for each session. But once the group members take more ownership of the planning, they can direct it more ("We need more work on the next level of work—can you design a lesson around that for us next time?" or "We need to learn more about assessment practices—what are the research findings about that topic?").

Turning important decisions over to the group is a way to signal that network members own the work. In Cambridge, when the school committee wanted to join a rounds visit, we turned the decision over to the network. It respectfully said no and arranged for another way to share the work. Similarly, in Ohio, a member of one district at first asked us permission to invite additional district representatives to join the network. We deferred to the network. After he made his case and the group agreed to his request, he sighed and gave a heartfelt, "Thank you, colleagues." After a sample rounds session in Iowa, potential network members decided how often they would do visits and what kinds of follow-up they wanted. They also spent a great deal of time figuring out the details of who would be eligible to participate in the network (e.g., what about people who initially turn down the invitation but then reconsider, or those who start in the network but then switch jobs and move to another part of the state?). This time was well spent because people were beginning to take ownership of the group through this conversation.

■

Tips and Takeaways

As you navigate the terrain of the rounds network journey, remember that people get better at the rounds process over time—including the facilitators. Anticipate this and view your learning curve as a resource rather than a liability. Dilemmas abound: Who decides what? How much structure does the network need early on? What variation from rounds is innovation, and what is deviation? If I show my own learning and questions, will I look like a model learner and engender trust, or will I look incompetent? We hope this chapter has anticipated some questions and provided a starting place for you to answer them. We're certain, however, that those who engage in rounds will generate both new questions and new answers. Trust the network and trust the rounds process to help you find your way. The practice is powerful and messy and fun and challenging. Here are a few tips:

- *Model the work*, and *be explicit.* In everything you do, you're trying to model the kind of practice you hope to see in classrooms and school systems. Experiencing powerful learning will go a long way to helping the network participants develop a common understanding of what powerful learning looks like. We have, however, learned the hard, slow way that modeling is necessary but not sufficient. Learners, including adult learners, need explicit instruction as well, including clear expectations about taking back what they're learning (both content and process) and applying it to their own practice. For some network participants, it never occurs to them to use a protocol that they've experienced as part of rounds in their own everyday work—until someone mentions it, encourages it, and even expects it. Learners also benefit from an opportunity to name what they have learned and reflect on what has helped or hindered their learning.

- *Expect individuals to have different needs and preferences.* Facilitators working with adult learners are not immune to the great teaching challenge of participants with varying levels of experience and expectations. It can be hard to find the balance of meeting individual needs and moving the whole group forward. For example, some people want ideas of what to do tomorrow, while others want to think about long-term learning.

Every group will have some of each kind of learner, and it's helpful to try to provide something for both of these groups. People also bring different facility with the rounds practice. Some have never talked about practice with colleagues; others are part of multiple networks or lead staff development themselves. Some people will ask questions when they're confused; others won't. It's important to attend to all the learners in the network. Deliberately teaching the four elements of rounds, attending to norms of behavior and communication, and providing clear structures for learning will ensure that everyone moves forward.

- *Help more with questions than with answers.* Participants thrive with different levels of support and struggle. Some people want to be told what to do, while others want to figure out what to do, or at least can tolerate a little more ambiguity. Facilitators must resist the urge to provide answers— this urge can be strong and seductive, as it makes the participants feel better in the short term and makes facilitators feel competent and needed. Instead, allow participants to struggle while you provide enough support and reassurance that if the participants engage long enough and deeply enough, they will start working out their own answers.

- *Maintain vigilance about sticking to descriptive evidence.* Over time, network participants will improve their ability to stay in a descriptive rather than evaluative mode. They will also get sloppy about the practice, particularly when in small groups. Old evaluative habits are deeply ingrained in educators' observational muscle memory. Facilitators can help by anticipating this slippage and by doing reminders and practice tune-ups periodically throughout the network's meetings, even with experienced networks.

- *Less is more.* We have made the mistake of jamming in so many interesting experiences that we have to skimp on the time for talk and reflection. Consequently, although we have "covered" a lot of territory, the participants have lost the opportunity for participants to consolidate their learning, personalize it, and actually learn. We continue to remind ourselves that less truly is more. Go for depth over breadth and build in time for reflection and sense-making. Learning is about quality, not quantity.

PART 3

Rounds and
Systemic Improvement

CHAPTER 8

Learning from Rounds

The district leadership team—principals, lead teachers, and system administrators—has been engaged in instructional rounds for nearly a year. They meet monthly, at a time previously scheduled for principals' meetings, at a school site, and they spend the better part of the day working on instructional issues related to the district's overall improvement strategy. The principals and district leaders have developed their personal theories of action and have discussed them with other members of the leadership team. The team members report that they have made real progress in their own understanding of what they are looking for in classrooms, and there is an emerging language for describing what high-level instruction looks like. Team members also report that their work is more satisfying and that their common meeting time is more productive around instructional issues.

At the most recent school board meeting, a board member turned to the superintendent and deputy superintendent and said, "I have some concerns about this rounds process that we keep hearing about. I understand that you're very enthusiastic about it, but it seems like an awful lot of time away from the real work of running schools. Isn't there a quicker way to learn what you need to learn? I'd rather see the leaders in this district making improvements in their own schools rather than touring another school in the system every few weeks."

After the meeting, the superintendent turned to the deputy and said, "I think we need a better argument for why we're doing this work."

The rounds model works, we have argued, to the degree that it meshes with a system-level strategy of school improvement and to the degree that it reinforces mutual accountability relationships between students, teachers, and administrators. If rounds is regarded as an activity— just one more thing that educators have to fit into an already overcrowded schedule—then it will probably go the way of most good ideas about school improvement. It will gently sink into disuse and oblivion. At the same time, it is an unfamiliar practice to most people who are used to working in and around schools, and systems typically don't take easily to new practices. The situation in the aforementioned district is not that unusual, in our experience. People begin to master instructional rounds, they begin to see the benefits of it, they recognize the seriousness and difficulty of the problems that the practice uncovers in their own work, but they find it difficult, even after some experience, to state the rationale for doing it.

The rationale for rounds was succinctly stated by Paul Toner, the dedicated past president of the Cambridge, Massachusetts, teachers union and now the vice president of the state union, who participated as a member of the Cambridge Leadership Network during its first year. When we began visiting schools in Cambridge, Paul, at his own initiative, would visit teachers in the schools prior to the visits and address their questions about the process. He would say, in his down-to-earth way, "This is a way of making administrators smarter about the work of teaching, and anything that does that can't hurt."

Logical as this may sound, it is not uncommon in districts undertaking instructional rounds for people to question the practice. That it should be controversial to think of schools as learning organizations for adults as well as for students is an interesting commentary on American school culture and on the status of teaching in the broader society. But this situation is not unusual. We do not flinch when law firms, accounting firms, consulting firms, and other knowledge-based organizations set aside time for their employees to attend to their professional learning—indeed, they are *required* to do so by their management and by their professional associations. Why, then, should it be controversial to argue that people who organize, run, and teach in schools should take time from their regular work schedule to make their practice more effective? Perhaps the school systems and the public that surrounds them are just now recognizing that functioning effectively as an educator requires continuous learning over one's entire career. There are many ways to continuously learn and make instruction more effective. We think that rounds is a powerful way for doing both, and in this book, we have tried to show what that looks like.

In this chapter, we return to questions we started the book with—why and how do rounds lead to systemic improvement? The theory of action behind rounds often makes best sense to people after they have engaged in instructional rounds networks for several months. Before launching a network, the theory sounds good, but is so disparate from the participants' past experience that it looks more like activities than like a professional practice, and the distinction between the two is not clear. Instructional rounds is based on a set of professional-learning principles that we have developed and, in conducting rounds, later refined with our colleagues in the rounds process. These principles can be used to build the rationale for rounds as part of a more general process of learning and improvement in school systems. They can also be used to develop and test your own theory of action about rounds. This chapter examines the principles, drawing upon material from each of the previous chapters, and ends with our theory of action of how rounds leads to learning and to more effective teaching and leadership practice.

PRINCIPLE NUMBER 1: *We Learn to Do the Work by Doing the Work, Reflecting on the Work, and Critiquing the Work*

As noted in the earlier section on the instructional core, putting instruction at the center of school improvement grounds decisions about structure, process, and resource allocation in the actual work of teachers and students in classrooms. The central question about any administrative or policy decision should always be, "In what way does this particular decision enable or constrain high-level instruction in these particular classrooms and schools?" This question can be answered only by examining firsthand what is actually happening in classrooms, by engaging in serious analysis and discussion of what the next level of work is in classrooms, and by trying to bring broader organizational decisions into alignment with what we consider to be high-level instruction. Learning in rounds moves continuously back and forth from the particularities of practice in the classroom to the more general patterns of practice across classrooms to the organizational conditions that promote and sustain good practice, and back again.

There is only one way to learn how to do this work, and that is by actually doing it. Rounds is a practice and practices are learned by practicing. This means that practitioners must have an opportunity to do the work, to experience the initial awkwardness of adapting their actions to unfamiliar protocols, to reflect on the work, to express their feelings and understanding about the work, and to critique their own practice. Simply doing the work without reflection and critique means that the questions and concerns that individuals have about the work go undiscussed and unanswered. When big questions go unanswered, the work becomes routine and pro forma, but this general principle is often hard to understand except in the context of specific instructional problems and specific teaching practices. Many observations could be interpreted as either descriptive or normative (table 8.1). For example, some people will hear the statement "more boys than girls participated in classroom discussion" as a description of a pattern of classroom interaction, while other people will hear a judgment about inequality of access to learning in the classroom.

For example, one of the biggest issues that educators have in the early stages of rounds work is what kind of language to use in describing the teaching. Rounds networks create strong norms around the use of descriptive rather than normative language in discourse about instruction, but this general principle is often hard to understand except in the context of specific instructional problems and specific teaching practices. These and many other dilemmas typically emerge in early discussions of classroom observations. Questions about whether such statements are descriptive or normative become tangled up with some practitioners' queasiness about appearing to make judgments about teachers' practice, and they raise doubts about whether it is possible to make value-neutral statements about teaching in the interest of accumulating a body of evidence.

In working with practitioners on these issues, we try not to give them direct answers to the kind of questions that they raise, but to get *them* to reflect on *why* these questions are important, *why* they are problematical, and *how* they contribute to their understanding of instructional improvement. What we choose to observe in classrooms, at least initially, is a product of who we are, what our commitments are, what our prior experience tells us is important, and how we have used the language in the past. We try to help practitioners understand that creating a common language for describing and drawing inferences from instruction requires them to question their own categories and their own language and to use this reflection to create a common understanding of what is important with their peers. So, instead of telling practitioners that there is a right or a wrong answer to their concerns about descriptive and normative language, we try to get them to say why they chose to observe certain things in the classroom (and not others) and how their observations compare with others in the same classroom. We pose the question "How could you agree on what is important in this context, and how would you observe it?"

TABLE 8.1   DIFFICULTY IN INTERPRETING CLASSROOM OBSERVATIONS

Observation Statement	Descriptive Sense of Statement	Normative Sense of Statement
More boys than girls participated in classroom discussion.	Refers to a specific pattern of classroom interaction	Calls attention to inequality of access to learning
The teacher seemed to call on the same five or six students throughout the observation.	Refers to patterns of participation	Refers to the teacher's lack of attention to these patterns
Students carried on a discussion of a book without referring directly to the actual text.	Refers to the content of the discussion	Suggests that rich discussions should refer to the text
Students were unable to explain why they were doing a particular science experiment.	Refers to students' interpretation of the task	Implies that the task was poorly explained and understood
Students were organized into groups in the classroom but the nature of the tasks they were asked to do was mostly individual.	Talks about classroom organization	Judges the teacher's understanding of group work

Obviously, you cannot address these detailed questions without actually engaging in instructional rounds and reflecting on it. It is the practice of rounds that produces the juicy questions, and it is the practice that helps convert these questions into individual and collective learning. Most of the learning that goes on in rounds is *not* in the prior discussions or in getting ready to do rounds, although these things are important. Rather, it is in doing rounds itself and in staying with the troubling questions that doing so raises.

PRINCIPLE NUMBER 2: *Separate the Person from the Practice*

One durable legacy of the culture of atomized practice in schools is that most educators believe that their practice is an inherent part of themselves; it is a part of their identity as educators and it is more or less inseparable from who they are.

Hence, discourse around people's teaching and leadership practices treads lightly around differences. Most differences are attributed to matters of "style," which is a polite and anodyne way of saying that one practitioner has no business questioning another practitioner's practice because, after all, we are all interested in achieving the same result, and we just get there with different methods.

Make no mistake, the practice of rounds flies directly in the face of this belief system. We could be polite and say that each participant is entitled to his or her own view of effective practice and that rounds is simply a way of "sharing" our different styles with the goal of mutual respect and understanding. But this is definitely *not* what rounds is about, and to state its purpose in that way is to trivialize it.

Rounds is based on the highly contentious and problematic assumption that for schools to improve systemically, they have to develop *shared practices* and a *shared understanding* of the cause-and-effect relationship between teaching and learning. To characterize differences in practice as matters of taste or style, having little or no consequence for student learning, is to trivialize the importance of teachers' practice and its cumulative effect on student learning.

Furthermore, the view that practice is a matter of individual taste is profoundly antiprofessional. Professionals are not people who act according to their individual idiosyncrasies and predispositions, but people who subscribe to a common body of knowledge and a set of practices that go with that body of knowledge, and who use mastery as the basis for determining who gets to practice. We ask participants in rounds to imagine that they are on final approach on a flight to the local airport, when the captain comes on the intercom and says, "You are going to notice something different about this landing. I have always wanted to try this without the flaps." Or in your final presurgical conference with your cardiovascular surgeon, the doctor says, "I had an epiphany driving into work this morning, and I've decided to do your procedure the way I learned it in my residency in 1972." These intentionally extreme examples illustrate the point about what it means to be a professional. In each of these cases, if the professional in question does any one of these things, they will be called an ex-professional.

Professionals are people who share a common practice, not people whose practices are determined by taste and style. Furthermore, the only way to *improve* your practice is to allow yourself to think that your practice is *not* who you are. It is, instead, a way of expressing your current understanding of your work, your knowledge about the work, and your beliefs about what is important about the work. All these things can change—*should* change, if you are a professional—as your knowledge, skill, expertise, and understanding of your work increase. If you believe that you *are* your practice, the likelihood that your practice will change in response to new knowledge and insights is minimal. In addition, you can maintain all the values and commitments that make you a person, and still give yourself permission to change your practice. Your practice is an instrument for expressing who you are as a professional; it is not who you are.

Part of rounds, then, is to delicately, but insistently, separate people from their practices. We do this essentially by objectifying their practice and by asking them to describe their practice and codify it in a theory of action, and then we encourage them to test that theory against the daily realities of their work, continuously modifying it in the face of new evidence on its effect. We also encourage participants to treat other people's practice in the same way. We deliberately discourage language that refers to people's "style" of teaching or leadership, and we ask people to use descriptive language in the way they characterize each other's practice. These are not easy things to do. Confusing people and practice is deeply rooted in the culture of schools, and it is especially resilient because it resides in the beliefs and the language of school people. We speak of "gifted" or "natural" teachers, for example, without ever thinking about the implications of that language for how people improve their practice. If practice is a gift that falls out the sky onto people, then the likelihood that we will improve practice at any scale at all is minimal. There are only so many sunbeams to go around, and there aren't enough for everyone.

The premise of the rounds model is that *practices are learned* through the application of knowledge and skill to concrete problems, and that we get better at our practices by engaging in detailed analysis of whether the results we are producing with students are consistent with what we believe we are trying to do. The gap between what we are trying to do and what we are actually doing is where we learn. Understanding that gap requires us to treat our practice as something that can be changed, not an indelible part of our personality.

PRINCIPLE NUMBER 3: *Learning Is an Individual and a Collective Activity*

Some teachers engage in learning about their own practice all the time. Not everyone, however, has the same predisposition to learn and develop over the course of a career. So if we value individual learning exclusively in the way we organize teaching and professional development, we aggravate the problem that has stimulated the need for school improvement in the first place: We increase the variability in the quality of student learning among classrooms. Individual learning is good for individuals; we should do nothing to discourage it. Individual learning, however, is not always good for organizations, if the problem you are trying to solve is not just the performance of individual teachers but also the variability of students' learning across classrooms. If the *school* is the unit of improvement, then individual teachers have to work across classrooms to generate improvement. One classroom at a time won't work. Until recently, professional development in schools and school systems was relatively unorganized. Individual teachers enrolled in programs of their choice with little attention to the cumulative effect of their learning on the organization as a whole. What was good for individuals, the theory went, must be good for the organization. We now know that this model of professional development not only doesn't lead to cumulative improvement of schools, but in fact may aggravate the problem of variability in practice among classrooms.

The rounds model is designed to move schools and systems from these highly individualized practices of learning and professional development to more collective practices aimed at cumulative improvement at scale. Making this transition requires educators to move from thinking of learning as an individual process to a collective one. While individual learning is important, it is the accumulation of that learning across classrooms and schools that improves overall learning and student performance.

The rounds process explicitly models the movement from individual to collective learning by putting people in teams for observations and discussions, by engaging people in activities, by using protocols that require people to construct a common language for describing and analyzing what they observe, and by generating collective commitments for action on instructional issues. The products of this work are collective and are meant to model how individuals working together with a common set of processes and protocols can produce a common body of expertise and knowledge about their practice.

PRINCIPLE NUMBER 4: *Trust Enhances Individual and Collective Learning*

One of the basic findings of research on organizational learning is that collective learning requires a safe space in which people can share their questions and understanding without fear of being judged harshly by their peers or their supervisors. In the absence of these conditions, people in organizations tend to suppress important information about their own practice or about problems they see in the organization for fear that speaking honestly will result in ostracism or retribution. Learning organizations have clear norms and processes that produce high levels of trust and candor among participants.

In rounds, we ask groups to create their own norms, and we periodically revisit those norms both to assess how well the group is doing against its own norms and to ask whether the norms need revision in light of the group's experience. As we have described earlier in the book, we insist on two norms at the beginning. The first is confidentiality: Participants are bound by the mutual obligation not to identify specific names, classrooms, or schools in their discussions of the work outside the rounds process. In order to feel that they can speak with candor, people need to believe that what they say inside won't be used to put them at risk outside. Another norm we insist on at the beginning is specifically about participation. One possible formulation that we have used is, "Everyone speaks once before anyone speaks twice, and practitioners speak before consultants and facilitators." We also provide regular feedback to groups on patterns of participation and engage them in discussions about their capacity to monitor their own participation and that of the group. Beyond these two basic norms, each group creates its own norms about process and content.

The research on trust in schools is clear on the basic finding that increased relational trust among individuals in schools is related to greater focus on instruction and higher student performance.[1] *Relational trust* is the highest form of organizational trust. It is based on a history of reliable, mutually supportive relationships within the school and is not conditioned on a specific exchange of favors or material rewards. Relational trust does not develop spontaneously in organizations, especially where, as in schools, the culture works against sustained collaborative work. The trust has to grow out of patterns of practice over time in which people learn that they can depend on each other to behave in predictable ways in high-stakes activities. For many teachers and administrators, exposing their practice to the scrutiny of others is about as high-stakes an activity as one can imagine.

The rounds process is designed to develop relational trust through repeated interaction around stable norms, processes, expectations, and protocols. In an important sense, the norms, processes, expectations, and protocols substitute for relational trust in the formative stages of building a professional network. They constitute a form of what researchers call *transactional trust*.[2] Transactional trust is simply an agreement that if you act in a certain way, I will also act in that way; if you default on your commitment, I get to default on mine. Transactional trust provides a kind of procedural safety net that people can use to sort out their relationships with each other—a set of predictable patterns to orchestrate people's behavior—while individuals are working on the more sensitive and difficult task of constructing relational trust. It is important to understand that the norms, processes, expectations, and protocols that we have elaborated here don't substitute for relational trust. They simply provide a predictable environment within which to build relational trust. The norms are not the trust; the norms make it possible to build the trust.

One of the most difficult issues we face in our work with practitioners is what we have already described as the "Land of Nice." One way educators have adapted to a culture in which one's practice is one's private property and not a collective good is that they have developed patterns of language in which they never say anything directly to each other that could be interpreted, implicitly or explicitly, as a criticism. Interestingly, this norm does not apply when people are out of earshot of their colleagues—they often say devastatingly negative things about their colleagues in those circumstances. The culture of nice makes it extremely difficult to institute norms of candor in the discussion of practice. People are generally carefully measuring their words, often using the passive voice, jargon, and indirection to avoid saying anything that might be perceived as negative.

We have learned that there is a complex relationship between trust and candor. In the absence of relational trust, only the most self-confident or brash colleagues will engage in candid discourse about their colleagues' practice. But the existence of relational trust doesn't necessarily result in candor. Learning how to talk candidly about one's own practice and that of others requires learning a new language—as we have noted, a primarily descriptive, not a normative, language. It also requires common norms of discourse so that when I speak to you in a descriptive discourse, what you hear is not a negative assessment of your work. In a culture of indirection, euphemism, and jargon, speaking directly in descriptive language can be interpreted as a hostile act. Hence, it is important that groups have clear, visible norms about the use of descriptive language in order to authorize people to use that language without being blamed for being hostile. Even when the norms are clear, people often revert back to the culture of nice when the problems get particularly sensitive, and this requires the group to take control of enforcing its own norms of discourse. It is courageous in these circumstances for a group member to speak up and say that the words are getting in the way of the meaning.

When outsiders periodically visit our network sessions, one of the first things they observe is the specificity of the language that people use to talk about instructional issues and the honesty and candor that people manifest toward each other in discussing sensitive issues. These patterns and practices do not come naturally to educators. They are learned behaviors. And they are largely countercultural behaviors in the present institutional context of schools.

PRINCIPLE NUMBER 5: *Learning Enhances Individual and Collective Efficacy*

Another robust finding from the research on organizations is that collective efficacy has a fairly strong positive relationship to organizational effectiveness.[3] Interestingly, individual efficacy inside organizations does not have a strong relationship to performance. That is, people's individual sense of their ability to influence student learning may predict their own performance, but measures of individual efficacy don't predict organizational performance very powerfully. On the other hand, individuals' perceptions of *organizational* efficacy—that is, their beliefs about whether they can collectively engage in powerful actions that influence student learning—do predict performance fairly well.

Part of the theory of action underlying rounds is that if you put people in regular situations where they have to observe, analyze, and predict what students will learn from the instruction they observe, then people will develop a strong sense of the cause-and-effect relationship between how teachers teach and what students learn. But people can do this as individuals without it having much benefit for the organization. It is always good if people understand their own efficacy and if they understand as individuals how to support the development of efficacy in others. But the research suggests that this is not enough for large-scale improvement. The ideas of efficacy have to percolate up from the individual level to the organizational level in order for efficacy to have a large-scale effect on student learning. Collective efficacy requires collective work and collective norms, not just individual understanding.

So instructional rounds tries to model the relationship between individual learning about efficacy and collective learning about efficacy by putting people in situations where they have to develop common norms and a common understanding about the conditions that produce their success. It's important to write down these collective understandings. When we ask teams to develop their theories of action around instructional improvement, we ask them to produce a wall-size graphic that explains the relationship between the elements of their strategy, and we ask them to explain it to their peers from other teams. The basic idea here is that the theory has to be understandable to others and that it has to represent a model of collective efficacy to be useful in school improvement.

THE THEORY OF ACTION OF INSTRUCTIONAL ROUNDS

When we ask participants in our instructional rounds networks to develop their personal theories of action and then to share them with their network colleagues and their colleagues in their home schools and districts, we are essentially asking them to do what we have just done in this chapter. That is, we ask them to lay bare some of the assumptions about the essential processes that underlie their work. At the core of the practice of instructional rounds is a key presumption. *If the adults who work in schools and in complex school systems are actively learning about the relationship between their work and the work between teachers and students in the presence of content, then support for improved instructional practice will increase and become more effective and the work of teachers and students will become more effective.*

When we say that adults are "actively learning," we mean, as we have sketched out in this chapter, that there are routine settings in which people can actively practice the knowledge and skills required to become more effective practitioners, since we learn to do the work by doing the work. We also mean the organizational and cultural conditions that surround the work are conducive to learning and development: *If people distinguish between their identities and their practices; if people associate their learning not only with their own growth and development, but also with those of their colleagues and the entire organization; and if trust and collective efficacy are at the center of the norms, then the conditions are conducive to adult learning, which is a prerequisite for instructional improvement.*

Our theory also suggests that learning and development of adults must be explicitly connected through organizational processes to the learning and development of students in classrooms. The connections here are largely through investment in knowledge and skill at the classroom level—investment that results in teachers' higher levels of understanding of the content and learning strategies of their students, increases in the level of content, and more active engagement of students in producing high-level cognitive work. *Instructional rounds works to improve schools and districts if it results in more focused investments in human skill and knowledge in the classroom.* Making administrators smarter about instruction doesn't make students learn more unless it results in new knowledge and skill in the classroom.

Consistent with our understanding of theories of action, these conditional statements are always subject to revision and specification in light of new evidence. Questioning the practice, as the board member did in the vignette opening this chapter, is not a bad thing. In fact, questioning is part of the practice. Each of our networks routinely questions and revises its rounds practice, including the norms, process, and protocols that form the backbone of rounds.

In the Cambridge Leadership Network, for example, the network revisits its norms and commitments once a year. Every year, the network members ask, "Is rounds worth all this time?" Every year, they ask, "Do we really need to go into schools? Maybe we've seen enough. Maybe we could spend less time meeting if we didn't go to schools." And every year, they recommit to the time, to the school visits, and to each other. Every year, they also make adjustments that respond to their needs. In the third year of the network, they decided they wanted to delve deeper into particular challenges they were facing in math. They wanted to hold on to the network, but also create space for more differentiated professional learning. They decided to add study groups to their rounds model and used their professional development time to break into small groups with a particular focus under the umbrella of math (e.g., special education, second-language learners, transition from middle school to high school). The groups designed and conducted their own learning and then shared that learning with colleagues in a formal presentation. Their modification to the theory of action above might look something like this: "*If the adults who work in schools and in the complex systems that surround schools are actively learning about the relationship between their work and the work that goes on between teachers and students in the presence of content,* and if they are given choices about what areas of expertise to develop, then they will deepen the group's expertise and *then the supports for improved instructional practice will increase and become more effective and the work of teachers and students will become more effective.*"

We expect their theory of action to change as the network members learn more about what helps them learn and what leads them to apply their learning most effectively in the schools they lead. Having a final theory of action isn't as important as having a setting in which to test your theory of action. This is a vital function of rounds—to provide the context in which the organization can develop and then refine a theory of action about how to improve teaching and learning.

■

Tips and Takeaways

In summary, here are a few key strategies to facilitate the learning that happens in rounds:

- *Move from individual to collective.* Instructional rounds is about moving the learning in schools and school systems from a primarily individual activity to a primarily collective activity. In the default mode, schools are characterized by isolated work in classrooms. The instructional rounds model is designed to move learning into a common space in schools and school systems and to make this learning accessible to everyone whose work affects classroom practice.

- *Separate people and practice.* By focusing on the descriptive voice in observing and analyzing classrooms, instructional rounds provides a way of separating the person from the practice. Professional learning occurs when individuals disconnect their practice from their individual identity, making changes in their practice in accord with feedback on their work while leaving their individual identity and commitment to teaching and learning intact.

- *Cultivate trust.* Trust is central to achieving high levels of learning and performance in schools and school systems. Developing a common language for describing and analyzing instructional practice and common norms for collective learning can create trust among individuals.

- *Build efficacy.* Repeated practice of instructional rounds creates collective efficacy among teachers and administrators around student learning, and collective efficacy is strongly related to student learning in schools.

- *Encourage questions.* Repeated questioning of the value of rounds in connecting organizational practice with teaching practice is something to be embraced, not avoided. Asking difficult questions about the practice itself is a primary means of improving it.

CHAPTER 9

Moving from Rounds to Large-Scale Improvements in Practice

There was a flurry of paper as network members pulled the "Powerful Teaching and Learning" document out of their binders. It was the latest rendition of the double-column chart that the group had started on its very first visit. One column listed "What students would be saying and doing" and the other column listed "What teachers would be saying and doing." People skimmed the sheet to remind themselves of how the document had changed since the last session when they'd added to it.

The facilitator then led the group through a process of relating the behaviors in this document to the behaviors they would like to see leaders around the district exhibit. Step by step, the group began asking what the superintendents would need to do to help principals improve their practice so that they could in turn help teachers improve their practice, which would lead to increased learning for students. "If your district is truly a learning organization, what would principals be saying and doing at meetings? What would superintendents be saying and doing?" People leaned in around tables to construct charts of "Powerful Leading and Learning."

"Well, my principal meetings are going to look different because of this network, that's for sure," said Rita, one of the deputy superintendents.

"You mean you're going to cover more about the instructional core?" a colleague asked.

"I mean I'm going to stop trying to 'cover' material and start thinking more about whether people are learning in those meetings," Rita answered. "If I want principals

to learn how to support teachers effectively, I have to stop just telling them how to do it." She paused for a moment and then reflected, "I don't know yet what I'll do instead. I guess I'll have to figure it out."

A superintendent from another district overheard Rita's comment and said with a grin, "If these network meetings are any indication, I bet you'll use a lot of chart paper!"

Our goal is to help schools and districts develop effective and powerful teaching and learning on a large scale, not just isolated pockets of good teaching in the midst of mediocrity. For that to happen, the learning from rounds must become more than just good individual professional development and must move beyond groups and clusters of educators working well together. Improvement at scale requires going beyond improvement with individual teachers or administrators to get to large-scale impacts at the school and district. Scaling up means that the ideas and experiences of rounds—the focus on the instructional core, the building of a collaborative learning culture, the use of ideas like theory of action to strategically focus improvement efforts—all have to become central to the core work of the district. Starting instructional rounds and successfully implementing it in schools and classrooms are necessary steps in our approach to large-scale improvement. But they are not sufficient. If these ideas and approaches stay on the fringes (where rounds is just another of the many improvement-oriented activities in a district) and do not trigger deep changes at the core, systematic instructional improvement cannot take place. Making changes in these organizational conditions—how the district in all aspects of its functioning supports instructional improvement—is the central challenge addressed in this chapter.

THE IMPACTS OF ROUNDS

With the help and engagement of educators in four states, we have developed, refined, and implemented the practice of instructional rounds and then refined it some more. By many measures, this rounds practice has been very successful. Principals, superintendents, and teachers routinely describe it as the best professional development they have ever had. Participants in superintendent networks value the experience enough to set up rounds among principals and teachers in their own districts. Each year, we hear of more states and districts that want to start rounds networks themselves. Participants in the networks report being energized by the collaborative learning opportunities offered by rounds and by its strong focus on classroom instruction.

We are thrilled by the interest, the enthusiasm, and the joint and mutual learning in which we and the rounds network participants have engaged. But does successfully doing rounds lead to large-scale improvements in instruction? We are often asked questions about impacts: Will doing rounds increase student learning? Will it raise test scores?

The short answer is—by itself—no. The rounds process is not a silver bullet that will singlehandedly lead to better outcomes at scale for students.

It is, however, a powerful accclerant of school and district improvement efforts. Its focus on what goes on in classrooms anchors improvement efforts in the instructional core and provides a key source of data and a powerful feedback loop to tell educators whether their systemic improvement efforts are actually reaching students. The collaborative learning approach used in rounds networks separates people from their practice and creates norms that make individual and organizational learning possible. Rounds specifically includes suggestions to visit hosts for feedback on how the school and district level can better support improving instruction. The process itself models a planning-doing-assessing improvement cycle that can be applied to all levels of practice, including the leadership and organizational changes that are needed to systemically improve instruction.

Yet all this will have a marginal impact if the ideas embodied and learned in rounds do not become central to shape how the district works to improve teaching and learning at scale. This chapter focuses on what we are learning about these impacts—about how rounds can connect with, support, and grow organically out of and into school and district improvement efforts. In the next section, we outline three broad areas that districts must address to improve how they improve teaching and learning at scale—focusing on the core, building a collaborative learning culture, and strategically focusing improvement efforts—and describe how successfully conducting rounds contributes to each.

HOW DISTRICTS BRING INSTRUCTIONAL IMPROVEMENT TO SCALE: MAKING CHANGES AT THE CORE

Districts trying to go beyond isolated pockets of excellence and bring good instruction to scale need to accomplish three interwoven tasks:

- Develop a clearly articulated and widely held and understood point of view on what high-quality teaching and learning look like—a view that is shaped by the best thinking available (inside and outside the district) about improving the instructional core.
- Build a collaborative learning culture that replaces the compliance orientation (for children and adults) typical of most districts, with one of engagement, collaboration, and continuous learning. To be successful in facilitating student learning and the higher-order skills of analysis, inquiry, and creative problem solving, districts must develop and encourage these same skills in adults.
- Develop and implement coherent systemwide strategies that support the kinds of teaching and learning that districts want in all their classrooms. This means building a theory of action that articulates their belief about how to most effectively improve instruction and student learning, focusing deeply on a few key strategies that bring their theory of action to life, and then aligning the allocation of human and financial resources and support and accountability systems to these strategies.

To achieve improvement at scale, districts need to make progress on all three of these conditions. Improvements in one or even two areas won't suffice. This requirement is similar to how improvements in only one of the three elements of the instructional core yield lopsided and limited gains. For example, a clearly articulated point of view about instruction without a collaborative learning culture can lead a district to conduct evaluative walkthroughs in which supervisors enforce teacher compliance to a checklist of teaching behaviors, but don't focus on the improvement of true teaching.

We have found that rounds naturally contributes to the first two elements and, with some thoughtful attention, can significantly support the third. At a very fundamental level, rounds is about developing a common understanding of good teaching and learning. Networks cultivate a collaborative learning culture. But those alone are not enough. You can have some pockets of people contentedly doing rounds, developing a shared view of instruction, and experiencing a collaborative learning culture. But you need the third element—how the district takes coherent action to systemically support good teaching and learning practices—to build on the first two and lead to districtwide impacts. Not surprisingly, this integrating and implementing aspect of improvement requires the greatest amount of work and the deepest changes in the leadership and organizational practices of the district.

Developing a Clearly Articulated and Widely Held and Understood Point of View on High-Quality Teaching and Learning

It may seem obvious that getting to scale with powerful teaching and learning for all students requires having and sharing a vision of what that should look like. If, after all, you don't agree on where you are trying to get, it is pretty challenging to get there. Yet we have worked, collectively and separately, in dozens of school districts where there was no common point of view on instruction, where ten educators from the same district could watch a fifteen-minute classroom video and have ten different opinions about its quality, ranging the full gamut from high praise to excoriation. Gaining an explicit and widely held view of what constitutes good teaching and learning in your setting is a first step toward any systematic efforts to scaling up quality. In the words of the great educational philosopher, Yogi Berra, "If you don't know where you are going, you will wind up somewhere else."

What Rounds Contributes to a Shared Understanding

Rounds keeps attention focused on the fundamental work of schools—the learning of students—and on all three aspects of the instructional core. Rounds enables educators to draw on external input and local knowledge in developing a shared understanding of teaching and learning at a detailed level and to test and refine that understanding. Rounds is also a powerful source of data that can inform and motivate teachers and administrators. As one teacher said, "Rounds helps us show why we need to change some of the things we've been doing. If you want to change people's behavior, you have to change their thinking. People are behaving in a certain way for a reason—so if you want to change their thinking, you have to give them reasons. The rounds process encourages reflective practice—it gives me and my colleagues a look at different thinking. If I see your thinking and your evidence, then I'll behave differently." As the network develops, its ideas about powerful instruction develop.

What Networks and Districts Can Do to Reinforce This Understanding

We have seen that the intensive, iterative, and collaborative focus on teaching and learning naturally accelerates a district's ability to get clear on its ultimate goal, student learning. Districts can enhance the effects of this by clearly and widely articulating their point of view on teaching and learning and making sure the point of view is known and understood beyond the group that is doing rounds. It should be known and used by everyone in the district who is involved in instruction—administrators doing evaluation and supervision, those responsible for professional development and testing, parents and students whose roles change as the level of instruction goes up, and so on. Involving more educators in rounds is one way to both build the district's shared vision of teaching and learning and extend its reach.

Building a Collaborative Learning Culture

Classrooms, schools, and districts are nested learning communities whose cultures are closely linked. Teachers who operate in a compliance mode with their principals are unlikely to create anything other than a compliance environment for their students. And as a former principal in one rounds network put it, "Principals cannot lead collaborative learning if they have not experienced it." Students are not likely to take risks, collaborate, learn together, and experience higher-order tasks unless their teachers are doing so. Recognizing these nested relationships helps leaders in a variety of roles take responsibility for leading learning.

What Rounds Contributes to a Collaborative Learning Culture

Rounds contributes to changing classroom, school, and district cultures in several ways. The network culture that is critical to the success of rounds provides a very concrete, experiential model of meaningful ways for adults to work with one another:

- The rounds network shows what kinds of time, resources, and organizational structures best support this kind of collaborative work. For busy educators who might think that collaborative learning cultures are a good idea in theory, but couldn't be implemented in their setting, rounds provides proof that with proper structures and focus, educators and their colleagues can commit to and benefit from collaborative learning.
- The rounds network models the "safe space" necessary for personal and organizational learning and helps leaders understand what's necessary to achieve it. It offers a place for teachers and administrators to set aside their usual hierarchical, compliance-oriented behaviors and try on another culture in which it is safe to be vulnerable and to learn. As one union leader put it, "It's the psychological safety of the rounds process that allows teachers to open up the doors and let people in—which is scary—and lets them see their work and be able to get that feedback in a nonthreatening way. It's usually not that way—it's usually threatening. This allows us to open up the craft in a way that we haven't been able to do in a long time."

- Rounds offers a set of norms and protocols that support the work by changing or replacing the default culture of isolation, idiosyncratic practice, and self-protection with a shared learning culture. As one network member said, "In shared leadership, there's sharing the struggle. So it's no longer just the classroom teachers' problem; it's not the principal's problem. It's bringing the whole slice of the district to share the issue, share the problem, share the struggle." As they deepen the work and start to see changes in classrooms and in leadership and organizational practices resulting from rounds, participants develop a belief in their collective efficacy, frequently in places where little existed.

What Districts and Networks Can Do to Reinforce This Culture

Districts can make clear that rounds as an approach separates people from practice and that rounds studies all levels of the organization in support of teaching and learning. It's not a process to fix teachers. District leaders can model this approach by being public learners themselves. Particularly in the mixed-role networks, thoughtful superintendents have accelerated the learning of their district members when they fully engage in the process and publicly share what they are learning.

Districts can encourage or "allow" these new collaborative ways of relating to one another to permeate and slowly change the district, not keep them isolated as separate microcultures (as in, "that's the way we behave and work together when we are doing rounds, but this is the way we behave the rest of the time"). This often takes time, since compliance-oriented, hierarchical relationships are strongly entrenched in most districts. In some districts with a longer experience with rounds and as the rounds work has taken off among principals, it has begun to trigger new ways of working with one another and with central office. In Cambridge, for example, principals and central office administrators use data collected in rounds to collaboratively make decisions about professional development goals for the district. These kinds of ripples represent important new ways of working with one another and inevitably run into obstacles as they bump into old roles and expectations. Leaders in districts and schools can secure these changes by demonstrating publicly their own willingness to embrace and adapt to new, more collaborative cultures.

It helps if leaders publicly make connections between how compliance with adults leads to compliance with kids. In one network session, a deputy superintendent for curriculum and instruction reflected on what principals need to do to encourage higher-order thinking skills in classrooms in a public "aha" moment: "If we expect teachers in classrooms to be talking less and having the students work more, then principals in their meetings with teachers have to do the same, and so do we at the central office." This galvanized her team to revisit the district's professional development structure and methods. Examples like this one show how districts can purposefully reinforce collaborative culture in order to support improvements in instruction.

Developing and Implementing a Coherent Systemwide Strategy to Support Teaching and Learning in All Classrooms

While we have found that the rounds process naturally helps in the first two tasks districts face—identifying a common vision for teaching and learning, and developing a collaborative learning culture—this third element, although just as important, requires some additional work. To maximize the impacts of rounds, districts have to strategically focus their approach to instructional improvement and make sure that rounds aligns closely with it. At the same time, those conducting rounds, while starting with and maintaining a consistent focus on what goes on in classrooms, must also look beyond classrooms. They must look at how the organizational decisions school and district leaders make can help or hinder the kinds of practices they are trying to develop in classrooms. To improve instruction at scale—moving from classroom-by-classroom work to systemwide work—rounds participants need to understand the connection between their daily decisions and practices and the larger picture of how the system is improving.

These two ideas—the leadership and organizational practices that emerge from the examination of classroom practices, and the district improvement strategies that usually come down from the central office—need to be intertwined. For rounds to help in this integration, a district needs to have—or be actively developing—a coherent and focused improvement strategy. It is the intersection of a clear strategy, a carefully thought-out theory of action, and an integrated rounds process that leads to systemic instructional improvement.

Making the connections between rounds and focused district improvement strategies is challenging because it requires integrating other elements (the focus and direction for teaching and learning, and the development of a collaborative culture) in ways that necessitate deep change in leadership practices—in many cases moving to areas with which district and school leaders are less familiar. Just as we believe that teaching causes learning, we believe that leadership and coherent district strategy create the conditions for good teaching and learning to take place.

Rounds can be a powerful tool for improving teaching and learning, but only if the leadership and organizational practices needed to support what has been identified as good teaching and learning are taken to scale.

What Rounds Contributes to a Coherent Systemwide Strategy

Rounds helps develop and implement a coherent strategy by modeling theory-of-action thinking and by increasing lateral accountability among educators. Rounds contributes to a coherent strategy by helping participants develop theories of action, encouraging the theories' use, and providing feedback on their effectiveness. Our rounds practice includes the following tasks:

- Requiring a district theory of action as either a ticket of entry or an early-stage activity for a network
- Supporting superintendents and district teams as they develop the district theory of action
- Modeling how to develop a theory of action specifically for rounds, asking participants to map out the if-then proposition that undergirds the relationship between rounds and increased student learning
- Asking participants to connect rounds to other district improvement strategies and to look at their theory of action for rounds work and other district improvement strategies side by side to ensure clarity and coherence between and among them.

The rounds process provides valuable feedback on district strategies by reflecting on whether and how the hoped-for results show up in classrooms. Observations in classrooms and the next-level-of-work discussion also suggest what might be missing in the strategy (or its implementation) and what would strengthen it. As one deputy superintendent said, "We had, at the district level, been working for several years on increasing teacher capacity to ask questions for higher-order thinking skills. When we did rounds, we saw that much of that had not made it into classrooms. Rounds showed that we still have more work to do and is giving us some ideas on how to do it."

What Districts and Networks Can Do to Reinforce This Strategy

Reinforcing systemwide coherence requires a clear district theory of action that includes a specific theory about how rounds contributes to and accelerates the district's improvement strategy. Put simply: You get more of a payoff from rounds if you have a strategy and use instructional rounds to reinforce it. The greater the clarity and focus of the district's theory of action before starting rounds, the better. For districts starting rounds without a theory of action, the sooner a theory is developed and the more tightly it is connected to rounds, the better. Rounds can then be a powerful data source—shedding light on how consistent your practice is (as superintendent or as a district) and how well you are working together as an organization.

Beyond that, districts need to look at how other systems align with the overall purposes of their strategy and with what they are learning about instruction from rounds—for example, how are supervision and evaluation, professional development, and hiring for teachers and administrators connected to any emerging vision of good teaching and learning? As a deputy superintendent put it, "Rounds reminds me of all the pieces that have to be aligned at the district level if we really want to be doing well with this in every school. We have some schools that are doing okay, but it's not because of anything the district is doing. We need the district to be paying attention to doing well with all schools."

Districts need to send a clear message about what is important and follow up consistently. A district that talks about valuing the quality of teaching and learning (and sometimes more specifically, of, say, teaching for higher order thinking skills for students) and then only holds principals accountable for quickly raising test scores and maintaining discipline sends a mixed message. Districts can also embrace the learning that comes from rounds. Recall the example in the theories of action chapter (2) when Cambridge rounds revealed some common concerns about mathematics instruction. Rather than respond defensively or hierarchically, the district saw it as a learning opportunity and chance to improve professional development.

GETTING TO LARGE-SCALE INSTRUCTIONAL IMPROVEMENT: WHEN AND HOW DOES ROUNDS WORK BECOME *THE* WORK OF THE DISTRICT?

If all this talk about what it takes to make deep change feels like a lot of work, it's because it is. Getting all the organizational conditions of the district to support the instructional core in the classroom is not just hard work; it is *the* work of educators. We close with key ideas that we, and the rounds participants with whom we work, are learning about the most powerful levers to support this change over time.

Involve the Right People

For rounds to be more than a marginalized activity that provides good learning for some, and for it to be central to the work of the district, authority figures and key stakeholders must be engaged—and the sooner the better. This is why the networks in which we have started instructional rounds have always included superintendents. When we were invited to work with mixed teams in Ohio, we insisted on superintendent involvement, and we also recommended that teachers, principals, and union leaders be involved. Without this mix of stakeholders, rounds will have a tough time getting to the core. We have not yet engaged in teacher-only rounds networks; we expect they would provide important individual and group learning, but have a considerably harder time getting leverage for district change unless they were part of a system of networks in a district.

Not only do the right people have to be involved initially, but more and more people need to be pulled in over time. Since rounds is highly experiential learning, an explicit part of taking it to scale is engaging increasing numbers of educators in a school or district in the process. One way that two of our networks have done this is to hold a "plenary" session. Network participants bring colleagues from their schools or districts (e.g., principals bring teachers and assistant principals; superintendents bring central office and school-based personnel) to a onetime session that includes an overview of the instructional core, video observation of classrooms, and some team-based work (e.g., assessing internal accountability, drafting a theory of action). These sessions have allowed networks to share the rounds practice and generate excitement as well as plans for starting new networks in the system.

Provide Explicit Expectations for Individual, Group, and System Learning and Follow-up Applications

We've discovered that we need to be more deliberate in mapping out expectations with networks. However, it's important to figure out the balance between requirements for everyone from day one and expectations that develop over time from examples in individual practice or from the collective will of the network. Below, we offer a few examples of how expectations have developed in different networks.

Our networks have not always included expectations for what the host school should do once the network leaves. For example, in one network, without any clearly agreed-upon network expectations or established practices about follow-up, when we asked what the host principal had done with the data after the visit, we got widely varied responses. One principal left up the sticky notes containing the raw data from the visits (data that tracked the low levels of questioning behaviors visitors found on Bloom's taxonomy) and brought teachers into the library to see the data. Another principal hadn't—a month later—said anything to the faculty. One had shared the positive feedback with his staff and hoped at some point to get to sharing what might be seen as disconfirming. All three responses were reported back to the group, without real comment. In response, the network's think tank tuned its practice to increase follow-up connections to school and district improvement. Without clear expectations, whatever improvements happened at the host school or district were haphazard, idiosyncratic, and unsupported by the network—exactly the default culture that rounds is designed to address.

As a result of their positive experience in the early rounds work in Connecticut and Cambridge, many participants set up rounds in their own district (for Connecticut superintendents) or their school (for Cambridge principals) as a way to bring more of their own stakeholders into the work. Yet, many participants did not. Some leaders used the protocols and structures that we deliberately modeled to strengthen adult learning in their schools and districts. Many did not. Network members faithfully came and clearly valued their own participation, but in the absence of any clear message or expectation set by the network, they viewed it as powerful professional development for them as individuals. They were satisfied, but it was unclear—or left up to them—how and how much of their learning went further and to what extent they were expected to change their own practice. Furthermore, without clear expectations, there was no clear and structured support or sharing of their follow-up work. Superintendents who had elected to start rounds among the principals and teachers in their districts might talk about it over lunch with others, but it was on their own. Others who had used their learning about theories of action to formulate and publicize their own theories, and to ask principals in their districts to do the same, were similarly acting on their own.

On the other hand, when clear expectations for follow-up work are in place, not only are more powerful systemic ripples created, but those that are can be supported by the network. For the Connecticut network, those expectations have evolved over time and are currently in place. For other, more recently formed networks, the expectations were made explicit from the beginning. For instance, districts that wished to participate in year 1 of the Ohio Leadership Collaborative came in with an explicit commitment to develop and implement an in-district rounds model beginning in year 2. This work, which is now rippling out to affect hundreds of others and to align with strategic improvements in four urban districts, is structured and supported by the network. Districts share and get feedback on their implementation plans from the facilitators and their colleague districts and use each of the larger statewide network meetings to calibrate and improve their in-district rounds work.

Clear expectations for individual and group follow-up from rounds have other implications. If a principal, for instance, is expected to follow up on the suggestions for the next level of work at his or her school, there is—and should be—a clear expectation for support for the principal from the district and the network. However, network suggestions don't end there. By looking at the district's role in the next level of work, rounds requires that network members study each link in a district's theory of action to identify the learning and improvement demanded of leaders across the system. Participants look at the entire chain of a theory of action—the throughline that connects what goes on in the central office with the classroom—and recognize, together, that each person in that chain is implicated. Each one may need to learn new ways of operating to shift the system to support improvements in the instructional core. Not only are the impacts greater when participants are expected to do something as a consequence of being part of rounds, but the mutual accountability and mutual learning grow dramatically.

Expect the Network to Learn over Time

Just as individual participants get better at rounds as they do it, networks grow over time, deepening and adapting their practice and learning together in increasingly powerful ways. We have seen that people come to rounds for a variety of reasons, like personal interest, the attraction of doing something that has status, being part of a concerted effort of a school or system, or seeking to learn how to improve student learning. Some are required by a system decision, say, to have all principals participate. Participants usually come with relatively little understanding of what they have gotten into and only realize later—through recursive practice—what they are learning. A frequent comment is, "I never understood what was meant by X [e.g., problem of practice] until I did it three times." The experience creates a virtuous cycle: As people do the work, they learn the work and get better at it. They learn more about instruction and their role in improving it. As they and their colleagues begin to implement ideas generated by rounds, they see small gains that lead to continued learning, experimentation, and further commitment. After some months of successful rounds, people often find that their reasons for participating have shifted and are more collectively aligned.

We graphically represent this with the improvement curve shown in figure 9.1. At early stages, participants are doing rounds mostly technically—following directions, learning the practice, doing elements because the participants are supposed to. At the next stage of rounds, as participants understand and engage more deeply, they are using rounds to change the culture. The real dramatic gains in this model come when the culture starts to drive the work. In this stage, it becomes clear to all participants that rounds *is* the work of instructional improvement, not something off on the side that gets done once a month.

Two examples from Connecticut—the longest-running of our networks—illustrate this maturation and continued development of collaborative culture. Several network members told the group they were concerned about the length of time before a revisit (two to three years). In response, the network decided that within a few months of a visit, two peer volunteers would follow up in person at the host's district.

There were technical implications for the network, namely, the need to develop (and tune) protocols for the revisit cycle, to figure out what would be done outside the network, and to decide how the network would learn about the follow-up. There were also deeper adaptive challenges related to the conscious choice to increase lateral accountability. Indeed, one thoughtful and long-term leader in the group initially opposed the follow-up peer visit: "I am already accountable to too many people; I don't want to add anymore." The group decided to move forward (and the early skeptic is now one of the strongest fans of revisiting). A second decision was to help superintendents make stronger links in the leadership practices that connect their work in the central office and what goes on in classrooms. Specifically, many in the network realized that having effective teams (senior leadership teams as well as other teams at all levels) was important in the implementation of their theories of action about instructional improvement. The network decided to use its annual retreat to learn more about teams, and then voted to add a team observation (by video or in person) to augment its classroom site visit protocol. Superintendents read about teams, participated in surveys and follow-up discussion about the effectiveness of teams in their districts, and began to coach one another on improving team dynamics.

Both stories show network learning and evolution over time. Both changes were nurtured by a data-rich, reflective learning climate. Their implementation (even

FIGURE 9.1   THE WORK OF IMPROVEMENT: FROM TECHNICAL TO CULTURAL

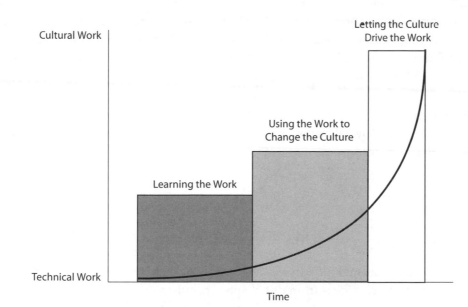

over initial opposition in one case) was possible, due to the strong connections and trust that had built among the superintendents. Over time, the network members have taken increased risks and opened up more and more of their leadership practice, showing how a network with a strong culture can creatively, courageously, and collectively improve leadership as well as instruction.

Expect New Forms of Accountability to Develop

Closely related to the improvement curve in figure 9.1 is a shift in the role that authority and accountability structures play in rounds. In many districts, authority can be a key to getting started. A superintendent or leadership team decides to do rounds, and principals and other central office personnel are in it. Or existing superintendent networks, as in Iowa, sign up to do rounds with "the Harvard team," and superintendents join. In the beginning, there is the expressed desire of the superintendents to do it "right"—to respond to the credibility and authority of the facilitators (and perhaps their network administrators). But over time, as successful rounds take place, we have seen this compliance to authority diminish and the culture of improvement shown in figure 9.1 take over.

As rounds culture takes over and participants see rounds as less about responding to authority and more about improvement, another powerful shift takes place as accountability becomes less vertical and more lateral. As rounds teams develop a greater sense of individual and collective efficacy, they are willing to hold peers more and more accountable—for maintaining the norms, for committing to the process, and for following up on peers' implementation of the next level of work. We have also seen shifts with what have traditionally been hierarchical in-district relationships. Although vertical accountability structures may still be in place, they are complemented by network-based mutual and reciprocal accountability systems, more driven by outcomes and common learning than rank and position.

■

Tips and Takeaways

Instructional rounds is not a magic bullet, but can help to improve learning and teaching at scale. Key ideas from this chapter include:

- Instructional rounds, by itself, cannot be expected to result in large, systemwide improvements in student learning and performance. Instructional rounds is a specific practice embedded in a larger system. It works best when it is coupled with a clear, widely shared district point of view about what powerful instruction looks like; a collaborative learning culture that values human skill and knowledge as a central feature of school improvement; and a clear, widely understood systemwide improvement strategy.

- Instructional rounds can accelerate large-scale instructional improvement by providing a setting for creating specific agreements on what constitutes effective instruction; serving as a setting for individual and collective learning; and contributing to the development and testing of a clear theory of action of systemic improvement.

- Instructional rounds is most effective as an accelerant to systemic improvement when it moves from being an additional activity to being *the work*. *The work* is the body of settled routines and practices that constitute the everyday responsibilities of people in an organization. To the degree that instructional rounds becomes a marginal or an optional activity, it is unlikely to be effective in advancing systemic improvement.

- Instructional rounds accelerates large-scale instructional improvement to the degree that rounds participants take control of the practice and change it to meet the demands of their work.

- Instructional rounds is a means of moving education from a collection of more or less independent practitioners nested in a bureaucratic structure to a profession, with a shared set of practices, a body of collective knowledge, and a set of mutual commitments that define professional accountability.

A Profession in Search
of a Practice

We began this book by outlining three main ways to think about instructional rounds in the context of the current educational reform agenda: rounds as an *organizational learning process* in which educators work systematically together in a collegial fashion to build the knowledge and skill necessary for instructional improvement; rounds as a *culture-building process* in which educators explicitly challenge the norms of privacy of practice and deliberately vague use of language to build and sustain a culture of instructional improvement; and rounds as a *political process* that is designed to strengthen and deepen the role that educators play in the broader school reform debate.

In the world of educational reform, educators are largely people to whom things are done. Knowledge of teaching and learning, no matter how promising it might be, seldom plays a visible role in the discourse of high-level policymakers in the same way, for example, that the latest medical knowledge plays a role in policy-making for health issues. When teaching and learning do enter policy debates, it is usually in the form of easily digestible sound bites, many of which have no basis in empirical evidence. Nor does detailed knowledge of teaching and learning play much more than a symbolic role in the discourse of high-level administrators in the education sector. People with a deep knowledge of how children and adults learn are seldom consulted about the details of the policies and the institutional arrangements that affect their work. Teaching itself is regarded by the public and by most people who participate in policy debates as a noble calling, a service to society, but not one that requires a particularly high level of specialized knowledge or technical skill. Claims that education requires a command of knowledge and skill comparable to other professions in society are typically treated in policy debates as special pleading by educators designed to fatten their paychecks.

Admittedly, as educators, we have largely done this to ourselves. We cling to a form of organization that makes it extremely difficult to employ our best ideas on any kind of large scale. We tolerate a kind of benign vagueness in how we talk about the core functions of teaching and learning that privileges good intentions over demonstrable effectiveness in our practice. We sanction unacceptably large variations in teaching from one classroom to another with rhetoric about teaching as "style," "art," or "craft." And we reinforce the public's stereotypes of teaching and learning as a knowledge-weak practice by largely refusing to exercise anything but perfunctory control over who gets to practice in classrooms and what happens to people who are demonstrably incompetent.

In the history of professions, social status and political authority accrues to occupations that seize it, not to those that wait patiently for public authorities to bestow it. Professions become professions by deliberately taking control of the means of production in their sphere of authority, by exercising strong influence and control over the terms and conditions of their practice, and by making judgments about what constitutes acceptable levels of knowledge and skill for practitioners. At this moment, education is perched precariously somewhere between an occupation and a profession, with a developing body of knowledge about learning and the conditions that support it, but with little or no professional infrastructure to parlay that knowledge into something resembling a professional practice that could influence the way children learn on a broad scale. At the same time, the policy system is bearing down on schools with increasing scrutiny and external pressure through systems of accountability and control that embody only the flimsiest understanding of learning and its organizational requisites. Policymakers don't particularly care about the state of professional knowledge in education, in large part because they don't have to care. The profession—as a profession, not as an occupation represented by competing, factionalized interest groups—doesn't command enough social authority for policymakers to listen to it or, more importantly, to respect it.

We have tried in this book, and in our own practice, to link instructional rounds as closely as possible to the daily-ness of organizing, running, and sustaining schools and school systems. We have tried to stay as close as we can to the instructional core on the theory that building a powerful practice of instructional improvement requires steady, routine, and systematic immersion in the demanding work of classrooms. There is a risk, though, that in focusing so much attention on instruction and in organizing our practice so much around the instructional core, the broader significance of the practice will be lost and, as with so many promising educational practices, it will be neutered and domesticated by the institutional structure of schooling. The commitment to staying close to the instructional core has to be accompanied by an equally strong commitment to the broader purpose of building a professional practice around instructional improvement.

At its foundation, instructional rounds is an attempt to build human agency in the field of education by building a common commitment to continuous adult learning that will be reflected in the work of adults with children. *Human agency* is the capacity to exert control over the terms and conditions of one's learning. It is impossible for schools to respond to the increasing pressure from policymakers and society at large for accountability without dramatically increasing human agency in adults and children around learning. It is possible to "do school," in the bureaucratic sense of holding class, following the curriculum, and mastering procedural routines and factual recall, without altering the current conditions of human agency. Asking more of schools, beyond simply "doing school," requires everyone to take greater responsibility and control over their learning.

A recurring theme in this book has been the importance of moving our conception of learning in schools from an individual good to a collective good. Instructional rounds moves the learning of adults and students out of the privacy of the classroom and into the public space of hallways, libraries, and conference rooms. It takes learning from something that individuals do or don't do in the privacy of isolated classrooms and makes it, first of all, an obligation. Rounds places demands on participants to engage with and learn from colleagues. Second, learning becomes something that people do together, in concert, in a way that is structured to improve their collective practice. In this sense, instructional rounds networks move the practice of individuals into the practice of professionals.

Thus, we offer this book with enthusiasm and hope. Working with committed teachers, principals, superintendents, central office personnel, state education leaders, and staff developers in four networks has inspired us. With their help and involvement, we have seen the practice of instructional rounds develop while supporting the critical work of improving the instructional core and becoming the kind of profession that educators deserve.

Sample Network Documents

EXHIBIT A.1
EXAMPLE DOCUMENT DISTRIBUTED TO SCHOOLS BEFORE
THE LAUNCH OF IN-DISTRICT NETWORKS

■

Professional Rounds: Questions and Answers

Q: *How is this process connected to the all-school improvement plan?*
A: Participants in professional rounds are members of the building's school leadership team. As such, they have responsibility for writing the all-school improvement plan and monitoring its implementation. The development of a high level of knowledge regarding effective, high-quality instruction is essential to the development of an effective plan because classroom instruction is the single largest factor in student achievement.

Q: *Does this process replace the CRT (curriculum review team) visits?*
A: Professional rounds will not immediately replace CRT visits. The process requires a full day in each building as it is a combination of observations and professional development for the group. Because of the number of buildings involved and because most of the group consists of principals and teachers, quarterly visits are impractical. The group will visit each participating school only once during the year.

Q: *Why are we doing this?*
A: A shared understanding of highly effective, rigorous instruction is essential if our students are to make dramatic gains in achievement. Decades of educational research have clearly identified the quality of classroom instruction as the single most important factor in student achievement. We need a deep, shared understanding

of what constitutes high-quality instruction that is consistent across the district. Rounds continually refines this understanding and places experts in each building. The rounds group comes to understand rigor, higher-order thinking, student engagement, and relevancy and distinguishes genuine high-quality instruction from "busy work" and, consequently, will be instrumental in making high-quality instruction the district standard. Rounds participants will help focus attention on the most effective strategies for inclusion in the building's all-school improvement plan.

Q: *How many people are involved in the rounds visit?*
A: This will vary somewhat. For the smaller groups of schools, the network has approximately twenty-five to thirty people, including two teachers from each building, the principal from each building, and other administrators. For the larger group of schools, the total number may be around forty to forty-five. No more than six people visit any single classroom at one time (usually it is four or five people), regardless of the overall size of the group.

Q: *Will every classroom be visited?*
A: A typical rounds process will involve multiple visits to every regular classroom in the building. Four or five people visit at the same time for about twenty-five minutes. Classrooms are visited two to four times each by such teams. If the building is very large, it may not be possible to visit every classroom, but this is the goal.

Q: *What will I need to do in preparation for a team visit?*
A: No special preparation is necessary. It would be thoughtful to provide four or five chairs or desks for the visitors and any handouts or assignments the class is doing during the visit.

Q: *Won't such a large group be disruptive to my class?*
A: Classrooms continue to function normally, in our experience with rounds. The group will be unobtrusive if you are doing whole-class instruction. If students are working in groups, members of the team may visit with groups and ask about what they are doing. We have found that students generally work harder and process their work more deeply with caring observers present.

Q: *Can I opt out?*
A: No. The days of isolated instruction, in which teachers can close the door to outsiders and work independently, are gone. Transparency of teaching and collaboration are crucial to dramatic improvements in student achievement.

Q: *How will you create an environment that respects psychological safety?*
A: The primary purpose of rounds is the professional development of the visiting team. Its business is not to judge the effectiveness of teachers, but to differentiate the practices that engage, challenge, and result in student learning from those that are less effective. The visiting team members are

essentially learners themselves. This is not an evaluative group out to get anyone. The group's focus is developing a deep understanding of *what is working for our students* and sharing this information widely. *Who* is doing what is not part of the discussion. As an observational exercise, rounds discussions omit judgmental information about individual teachers.

Q: *Can I file a grievance if my principal uses the feedback for my formal evaluation?*
A: It is virtually impossible that a principal could correlate information about a particular observed data point to a particular teacher. It is also a norm of the group that information about the building observations, especially observations of its individual teachers, is confidential. In the unlikely event that any information from rounds observations ever found its way into a formal evaluation, it would be stricken.

Q: *What are the norms the group uses?*
A: While many of the norms pertain to the internal functioning of the group such as "cell phones on vibrate" and "allow everyone in the group to share their data," the group also has a strict confidentiality norm that no one discusses any specific observations with anyone outside the group meeting. In addition, no classroom is ever referenced by teacher name or room number during the internal discussions. General results, feedback, and recommendations for the building are shared with the building's leadership, but no individual classrooms are ever discussed in these consultations.

Q: *Will any member of the group share individual feedback to my principal?*
A: No. This is a violation of the norms of the group. The group understands that this would be a violation of the trust of the schools being visited and would seriously damage the group's credibility.

Q: *Is there a formal agreement between the union and the administration about this process?*
A: Yes. Both the union president and union vice president have been involved in this process from the beginning. Both have participated in visits to buildings in various districts around the state as well as the discussions that followed the visits. The process has the enthusiastic support of union leadership as a methodology for increasing both the professionalism of teaching and the responsibility of teachers in school improvement.

Q: *How is the problem of practice determined?*
A: The school leadership team decides on the problem of practice. In general, this should be a major component of the school's improvement plan.

Q: *"Scripting" sounds like evaluation. How can I be assured that I am not being personally evaluated by this group?*
A: The team is "scripting" to collect evidence on the state of teaching in the building. This is necessary to ensure that conclusions and recommendations are based on specific evidence and not just feelings

or opinions. Before any evidence is shared with the entire rounds group, individual pieces of evidence from the observed lessons are transferred to dozens of sticky notes, which are attached to chart paper as supporting evidence for specific general observations. There is no reference to the grade level, room number, or teacher on the notes. The evidence from many classes is gathered together on the chart paper, which makes it impossible to assign a specific observation to an individual teacher.

Adapted with permission from Columbus City Schools, Ohio.

EXHIBIT A.2
FORM USED FOR APPLICANTS TO SUPERINTENDENTS' NETWORK IN IOWA

■

It's time to initiate your commitment to the ILA Superintendents' Network!

- Become a lead learner in a statewide community of learners
- Deepen your knowledge base through the work of an internationally recognized educator whose work will inspire and challenge
- Reflect on your leadership practice
- Create or refine your Individual Administrator Professional Development Plan

What is the Purpose of a Superintendents' Network?

Developed by Dr. Richard Elmore of Harvard University, the network model is intended to increase the capacity of superintendents to provide leadership for improved instruction. Networks give superintendents a safe space to grapple with difficult issues related to improving teaching and learning.

What is the ILA Superintendents' Network?

Each AEA will offer superintendents an opportunity to participate in a network. Coordinated through the Iowa Leadership Academy, networks are supported by the AEA statewide system and the Wallace Foundation. Collaborative partners: AEAs, SAI, IASB, DE.

The **Intent to Commit** form outlines expectations for participation.
Please discuss your involvement with your board.

Participant Expectations

- Attend all network meetings
- Host and participate in site visits
- Be an active and engaged learner
- Typical time commitment for meetings and visits combined is one day per month
- Honor network norms and display participant dispositions

Participant Dispositions and Skills

- Agree that confidentiality is non-negotiable
- Able to give and receive open and honest communication with colleagues
- Able to support one another through a change
- Able to confront brutal facts
- Willingness to hold each other accountable

Commitment forms are due to AEA _____ by *(date)*.
Please send signed form via fax, e-mail or U.S. Postal Service.

Intent to Commit

Name _____
(print or type)

District_____

In what area is your district focusing efforts to improve instruction? _____
Briefly, how are you going about this improvement work? _____
_____

Where can you be reached, even during the summer?
Phone _____ E-mail_____
Phone _____ Cell Phone _____

Assurances—Superintendent

I am committed to the ILA Superintendents' Network and our statewide community of learners.
I will:

- attend all sessions (1 day per month) and participate in follow-up implementation activities;
- host a visit in my district;
- apply learning in my leadership practice;
- actively engage in conversation with my peers; and
- honor the network norms and display participant dispositions.

Signature of Superintendent _____ Date _____

Assurances—Board

- We support the time commitment required of the superintendent to fully participate in the ILA Superintendents' Network, recognizing that this is a core part of the superintendent's work.
- We agree to engage in professional dialogue with the superintendent about his/her continued learning and how it relates to district and school improvement efforts and achievement in our district.

Signature of Board President _____ Date _____

Send or fax completed, signed application to:
Chief Administrator Name
AEA Address
Fax number
Commitment deadline: *(date)*, 4:00 p.m.

Questions? Contact *(chief administrator phone and e-mail)*

Used with permission of Iowa Leadership Academy Superintendents' Network

EXHIBIT A.3
PLANNING TEMPLATE PROVIDED TO FACILITATORS
BY STATE CONVENING AGENCY

■

Due Date: _____ Area Education Agency (AEA): _____

Iowa Leadership Academy (ILA) Superintendents' Network—Statewide System
AEA Planning Template

Directions: Complete and submit to [name] by [date]. This will allow time for network participants to be identified and given an opportunity to participate in decision making about their network.

Elements Common Across All AEAs

Element	Notes
Rounds model	All Iowa networks will use a *medical rounds model* in which superintendents participate in site visits to each other's districts. The host superintendent presents a *problem of practice* and shares his/her *theory of action* (an if-then statement describing the assumptions that have led to improvement actions). Network colleagues then observe classroom instruction and provide feedback using a descriptive, nonjudgmental protocol. Each participant is expected to host a visit within the network cycle. Appropriate professional development and process training are provided to participants. Facilitators help the host superintendents identify the problem of practice.
Consistent network	All networks will *maintain consistent membership* of practicing superintendents (as opposed to members dropping in and out, or conducting pair/triad visits, etc.). New members may be added to an existing network at the beginning of a school year if orientation and training are provided. Iowa Superintendents' Networks are for practicing superintendents only (not associate superintendents).
Participant commitment	All networks will use a statewide *commitment form* through which superintendents will indicate their agreement to fully participate and meet network expectations.
Facilitated process	All networks will use Harvard-trained *facilitators* (Iowa superintendents teamed with other educational leaders) to coordinate professional learning, organize visits, facilitate network conversations, and ensure fidelity to the basic principles of the model.

Elements Customized to AEA Context

Structural Elements (Facilitators create initial design; members provide input for changes in subsequent years through a "think tank" process.)	Considerations	AEA Network Decision
Time commitment	Typically one day per month is devoted to site visits and/or professional development.	
Frequency of site visits	Every other month allows for more time for professional development (on nonvisit months), but reduces number of districts visited.	
Size of network	Smaller networks the first year would allow facilitators to learn the work. Network must be small enough to allow each superintendent to host a site visit within the cycle. Recommended minimum size is six superintendents.	
Allowing new members to join	Not recommended midyear. Beginning-of-year considerations: existing relationships, numbers, trust, benefits of new perspectives, capacity to provide orientation and extra support, etc.	
Follow-up	Some form of follow-up is needed after host superintendent receives recommendations (promotes accountability and honors the work). Some networks use volunteers in triads to conduct a follow-up visit.	
Common POP with "through line"	Not recommended for facilitators to establish this. Should emerge from the problems of practice identified by individual members.	Yes/No If yes, what is the common problem of practice?

Norms of practice (Developed by the network participants; the following are example areas; your network may want to identify norms in different or additional areas.)	Connecticut Network Examples (For facilitator use only; do not share with the network, as we want norms to come from members.)	AEA Network Decision
Attendance	Everyone attends every meeting.	
Involvement	Everyone puts work out for discussion and engages in the discipline of practice.	
Respect for confidentiality	We agree to respect an individual's wishes not to discuss sensitive matters beyond the group.	
Candor and humility	We are willing to be candid about our best judgment and knowledge applied to the problems presented. We are also willing to acknowledge what we don't know.	
Attentiveness	Every member invests in listening.	
Mutual responsibility	We agree that we will use and abide by protocols and practices adopted by the network.	
Sharing	Materials produced specifically for members of the network may be shared outside the network with the permission of the author.	

Contact person in case of questions about this form: _____

Used with permission of Iowa Leadership Academy Superintendents' Network.

EXHIBIT A.4
HOW TO SCHEDULE A ROUNDS VISIT:
EXAMPLE OF NOTES FOR A HOST SCHOOL

■

Designate a rounds team who will take the lead on preparing for and following up from the visit. This team will help identify the *problem of practice* and decide how best to take the information from the visit and share it with the rest of the school. The team can consist of as many people as you'd like. Choose one to three members of the team to join our group for the rounds portion of the day. Some possibilities for membership on the rounds team include the assistant principal, members of your instructional leadership team, the building's union representative, and an instructional coach.*

A facilitator will meet with the rounds team or a representative of the team before the visit. At this meeting, we'll discuss what you'd like the network to focus on when we visit. This will be the problem of practice for our session. We'll also brainstorm ways you'd like members of the network to collect observation data. We may also discuss ways to engage faculty in this process if that would be helpful.

The following is a list of other details to attend to in preparation for a visit to your school. A facilitator will check in about all of these details, but you should also always feel free to call with questions.

Grouping

We do rounds in eight groups of about four or five people. We usually switch up the groups between rounds visits. Who is in which group is at your discretion. We usually mix it up, but if you want a specific kind of grouping, go for it. Be sure to assign the members of your host team to groups as well.

Scheduling Classroom Visits

You'll need the daily schedules of each teacher in order to make the rounds schedule (so as to target particular content areas if you choose and to avoid breaks and lunch and such). Here are some things to keep in mind:

- We get to as many different classrooms in a school as we can. In smaller schools, that's usually all classrooms. Classrooms are usually visited by one to three groups.
- When you build the schedule, it's great if you can make sure pairs of groups see some of the same classrooms. For example, Groups 1 and 2 would both see rooms 101, 102, and 103 (at

---

* We often give this document as well as a sample schedule, like the one in chapter 5, to a host school to help them prepare for a rounds visit.

different times) and might see different classrooms for their other observations; Groups 3 and 4 would see 201, 202, and 203, and so on. This will give the groups something common to discuss in the debriefing. Also, unless you are specifically focusing on a single grade, it can be useful to make sure groups see a range of grades.

- Each group usually visits four or five classrooms for twenty to twenty-five minutes. The time on the schedule includes passing time. If you have a large building, leave twenty-five minutes for the observation so folks have plenty of passing time.
- What grade levels each group sees is up to you and your staff. Sometimes, groups see all the classrooms in a particular grade level or across two or three adjacent grade levels (e.g. K–2, 6–8). Other times, groups see a wide range of grades. It's up to you, depending on what makes sense for your context and problem of practice.
- The schedule should include room number, grade level, and teacher's name (so we can be sure we're in the correct room).
- Consider whether there are other things you'd like us to observe, too, like team meetings or coach-teacher meetings or your own leading of a meeting.

The schedule for the day usually looks something like the following:

8:00–9:15	Welcome, focus on the problem of practice, and related professional development
9:15–10:45	Classroom visits
10:45–12:30	Debrief
12:30–1:15	Lunch
1:15–4:00	Next level of work and collaborative work

The schedule varies according to the start time of your school.

Logistics

To make everything go smoothly, and to save time, we will need to know the following information from your school:

- Start time (approximately 45–90 minutes before classroom visits begin). The start time varies by your school's start time, when it makes sense to start observing classes, and what our agenda is for the day—you'll make this decision in consultation with a facilitator.
- Where to go when we get to the school. Is there somewhere secure we can drop off bags and coats while we do rounds? Where are we gathering before we begin visiting classrooms?
- Parking. Is there somewhere in particular we should park? Do we need to fend for ourselves in finding a parking spot?

We'll also need the following:

- A room for us to use throughout the day. In most schools, the only available room that's big enough for our group is the library. Whichever room we meet in should only have us in it and should have doors that can be closed, in keeping with norms of confidentiality. We'll need the room for the morning welcome, debriefing, lunch, and approximately three hours of additional network time. Some schools reserve the library for our group's use that day.
- Copies of the rounds schedule for each participant.
- Copies of a map of the building if it's complicated to navigate.
- Markers, an easel, and chart paper for the day. We will also often need a computer hooked up to a projector and a screen for showing a PowerPoint presentation.

Other Preparation

Please plan on forty-two people for lunch, morning drinks, and snacks. Nothing fancy. We won't have much time for lunch, so box lunches or something that is fairly quick for self-serve will be helpful.

Signs at the entry of the school directing people where to go can be useful. Some schools post signs to identify classrooms as well.

Tips

After extensive experience with rounds, we have found the following tips to be useful in making rounds a productive, nonstressful activity for everyone involved.

- Be thoughtful about how to involve faculty in this process. Some principals informally poll faculty members about what they think the focus of the observation (problem of practice) should be. Others use formal data to pinpoint an area of weakness. They then share that with faculty to get input on the data that should be collected from classroom observations. Involving faculty early on can lead to a better-informed problem of practice and greater investment in working with the subsequent data from the observations.
- It's important to remember (and possibly let the rest of your school know) that the network is in the midst of a learning process as well. As the year progresses, we'll grow more skilled at observing for what individual schools ask us to observe.
- You might want to share the rounds schedule that lists group numbers with faculty at least a few days in advance of the visit. We tend not to include visitors' names when we share the schedule—groupings often shift at the last minute if someone can't come, and it can be more nerve-racking for teachers if they know that someone they know or the superintendent is coming. We do share the schedule, in part to be respectful so that teachers know when to

expect visitors, in part to make the visit less intimidating for teachers, and in part because it's really important that teachers confirm that they'll actually be in their classrooms when a group is scheduled to visit. If they'll be teaching somewhere else (e.g., outside or in the computer lab), we can go there—we just need to know to do that. You'll usually have to make some adjustments to the schedule after you show it to teachers. And then you'll probably have to make more adjustments right before the visit because . . . (see next point).

- *Something unexpected always comes up to mess up the carefully constructed schedule one or two days before the visit.* Expect this. Don't panic. So a teacher is going to be absent or the kids will be on a field trip, or whatever. No problem. We're school leaders. We make adjustments.
- Sometimes, the host team asks teachers to modify their schedules slightly so that the group can observe the classroom (e.g., push a break a little later, or teach math instead of literacy at 9:00). Such requests are entirely at your discretion. We definitely don't want to disrupt learning in your school, but if there's something you'd like our group to see and it's not scheduled to happen while we're there, teachers might be able to adjust schedules.
- Include your school's problem of practice and questions on the schedule to help remind us and focus our observations.

NOTES

Introduction

1. All names of districts, schools, and educators in the vignettes throughout the book are fictional. While based on our actual rounds experience, the vignettes are intended as illustrations, not as verbatim accounts.

2. For a description of the role that medical rounds plays in the education of physicians, see, for example, Gerard Hunt and Jeffrey Sobal, "Teaching Medical Sociology in Medical Schools," *Teaching Sociology* 18, no. 3 (1990): 319–328.

3. For a wonderful example of how physicians talk to each other about their practice, see Grant Cooper, *Hospital Survival: Lessons Learned from Medical Training* (Baltimore: Lippincott, Williams, and Wilkins, 2008).

4. Richard Elmore, Penelope Peterson, and Sarah McCarthey, *Restructuring in the Classroom: Teaching, Learning, and School Organization* (San Francisco: Jossey-Bass, 1996).

5. Our colleague Stefanie Reinhorn recently joined us to work with the Ohio Leadership Collaborative.

Chapter 1

1. The term *disruptive technology* comes from the work of Clayton Christensen, who first applied the term in the business sector in *The Innovator's Dilemma: When New Technologies Cause Great Firms to Fail* (Cambridge, MA: Harvard Business School Press, 1997). His recent book, *Disrupting Class: How Disruptive Innovation Will Change the Way the World Learns*, coauthored with Curtis W. Johnson and Michael B. Horn (New York: McGraw-Hill, 2008), applies the theory of disruptive innovation to education.

2. David Hawkins, "I, Thou, and It," in *The Informed Vision: Essays on Learning and Human Nature* (New York: Agathon Books, 1974), 49–62.

3. See David Cohen, Stephen Raudenbush, and Deborah Ball, "Resources, Instruction, and Research," *Educational Evaluation and Policy Analysis* 25 (2003): 119–142; Fred Newmann, BetsAnn Smith, Elaine Allensworth, and Anthony Bryk, "Instructional Program Coherence: What It Is and Why It Should Guide School Improvement Policy," *Educational Evaluation and Policy Analysis* 23 (2001): 297–321.

4. Walter Doyle, "Academic Work," *Review of Educational Research* 53, no. 2 (1983): 159–199.

5. David Hawkins, "I, Thou, and It," 50.

6. Doyle, "Academic Work," 185, 186.

7. One of our current favorite sources on this subject is Robert J. Marzano and John S. Kendall, *Designing and Assessing Educational Objectives: Applying the New Taxonomy* (Thousand Oaks, CA: Corwin Press, 2008). It is a much more current and powerful formulation of the traditional Bloom's taxonomy, and it is especially good in its treatment of the *self system*, that is, the student's orientation toward the meaning and significance of the learning, and the *metacognitive domain*, the student's capacity to reflect and self-monitor learning. It also deals well with the traditional cognitive domain.

Chapter 2

1. Chris Argyris and Donald Schön, *Organizational Learning: A Theory of Action Perspective* (Reading, MA: Addison-Wesley, 1978).

Chapter 4

1. The term *ladder of inference* comes from the work of Chris Argyris, Robert Putnam, and Diana McLain Smith, *Action Science* (San Francisco, CA: Jossey Bass, 1985). See also Peter Senge et al., *Schools That Learn* (New York: Doubleday, 2000), 68–71.

Chapter 5

1. For more on Bloom's categories, see Lorin W. Anderson et al., *A Taxonomy for Learning, Teaching, and Assessing: A Revision of Bloom's Taxonomy of Educational Objectives* (New York: Longman, 2001).

Chapter 6

1. The *principle of reciprocity* means that accountability must be a reciprocal process. For every increment of performance I demand from you, I have an equal responsibility to provide you with the capacity to meet that expectation. Likewise, for every investment you make in my skill and knowledge, I have a reciprocal responsibility to demonstrate some new increment in performance. This is the principle of *reciprocity of accountability and capacity*. It is the glue that, in the final analysis, will hold accountability systems together (Richard F. Elmore, *Building a New Structure for School Leadership*, Washington, D.C., Albert Shanker Institute, 2000). At the moment, schools and school systems are not designed to provide support or capacity in response to demands for accountability (Richard Elmore, "The Price of Accountability: Want to Improve Schools? Invest in the People Who Work in Them," National Staff Development Council, November 2002).

Chapter 7

1. See the standards for staff development and related research at the National Staff Development Council Web page, at www.nsdc.org.
2. Robert Garmston, *The Presenter's Fieldbook: A Practical Guide* (Norwood, MA: Christopher-Gordon, 2005).
3. Project Zero, *Making Teaching Visible: Documenting Individual and Group Learning as Professional Development* (Cambridge, MA: Project Zero, 2003).

4. Anthony Bryk and Barbara Schneider, *Trust in Schools* (New York: Russell Sage, 2002). For more on trust, see also Stephen M. R. Covey, *The Speed of Trust: The One Thing That Changes Everything* (New York: Free Press, 2008).

5. See Joseph P. McDonald, Nancy Mohr, Alan Dichter, Elizabeth C. McDonald, *The Power of Protocols: An Educator's Guide to Better Practice* (New York: Teachers College Press, 2007), 23–25.

Chapter 8

1. See Anthony Bryk and Barbara Schneider, *Trust in Schools* (New York: Russell Sage, 2002).

2. Ibid.

3. See Roger Goddard, Wayne Hoy, and Anita Woolfolk Hoy, "Collective Efficacy Beliefs: Theoretical Developments, Empirical Evidence, and Future Directions," *Educational Researcher*, April 2004, 3–13.

FURTHER READING
AND RESOURCES

A Taxonomy for Learning, Teaching, and Assessing: A Revision of Bloom's Taxonomy of Educational Objectives. Lorin W. Anderson et al. Columbus, OH: Allyn & Bacon, 2000.

Data Wise: A Step-by-Step Guide to Using Assessment Results to Improve Teaching and Learning. Edited by Kathryn Parker Boudett, Elizabeth A. City, and Richard J. Murnane. Cambridge, MA: Harvard Education Press, 2005.

Data Wise in Action: Stories of Schools Using Data to Improve Teaching and Learning. Edited by Kathryn Parker Boudett and Jennifer L. Steele. Cambridge, MA: Harvard Education Press, 2007.

Resourceful Leadership: Trade-offs and Tough Decisions on the Road to School Improvement. Elizabeth A. City. Cambridge, MA: Harvard Education Press, 2008.

Professional Learning Communities at Work: Best Practices for Enhancing Student Achievement. Richard DuFour, Robert Eaker. Alexandria, VA: Association for Supervision and Curriculum Development, 1998.

School Reform from the Inside Out: Policy, Practice, and Performance. Richard F. Elmore. Cambridge, MA: Harvard Education Press, 2004.

The Presenter's Fieldbook: A Practical Guide. Robert Garmston. Norwood, MA: Christopher-Gordon, 2005.

Leading Teams: Setting the Stage for Great Performances. Richard J. Hackman. Boston: Harvard Business School Press, 2002.

Making Teaching Visible: Documenting Individual and Group Learning as Professional Development. Ben Mardell. Cambridge, MA: Project Zero, 2003.

Designing and Assessing Educational Objectives: Applying the New Taxonomy. Robert J. Marzano and John S. Kendall. Thousand Oaks, CA: Corwin Press, 2008.

Cultivating Communities of Practice: A Guide to Managing Knowledge. Etienne Wenger, Richard McDermott, and William Snyder. Boston: Harvard Business School Press, 2002.

The "Usable Knowledge" Web site includes related articles and a video of Richard Elmore explaining the importance of the instructional core: www.uknow.gse.harvard.edu/leadership/leadership001a.html.

The "Is Yours a Learning Organization?" Web site includes a sample survey to assess your organization and a related video: http://harvardbusinessonline.hbsp.harvard.edu/flatmm/hbrextras/200803/garvin/index.html.

Protocols

The following book contains a great collection of protocols for school settings: *The Power of Protocols: An Educator's Guide to Better Practice, Second Edition,* by Joseph P. McDonald, Nancy Mohr, Alan Dichter, and Elizabeth C. McDonald (New York: Teachers College Press, 2007).

The National School Reform Faculty maintains an enormous collection of helpful protocols on its Web site: www.nsrfharmony.org/resources.html.

The Education Trust Web site includes the "Standards in Practice" protocol designed specifically to help a faculty or other group examine the task assigned to students. http://www2.edtrust.org/EdTrust/SIP+Professional+Development.

The Looking at Student Work Web site provides an excellent collection of protocols (and how-to advice) to help a group examine student work: www.lasw.org.

A Web site for Richard Hackman's book *Leading Teams* includes helpful coaching protocols: www.leadingteams.org/open/ToolsforCoaching.htm.

Videos of Teaching and Learning

We're always on the lookout for video to teach the skills of observing and moving up the ladder of inference. Many schools and districts develop video libraries of their own classrooms. Here are some other sources we've used for video clips:

We often show video from a book called *Content-Focused Coaching: Transforming Mathematics Lessons* by Lucy West and Fritz C. Staub (Portsmouth, NH: Heinemann, 2003). The book comes with videos of three teachers, all elementary level math. The videos also include some footage of coaches working with teachers.

Trends in International Math and Science Study (TIMSS) videos come as four CDs of 8th-grade math lessons—seven countries, four lessons per country. You may need persistence to track them down. TIMSS science videos are also beneficial.

For video of high school Humanities, see *Looking for an Argument* by Avram Barlow and Herb Mack (New York: Teachers College Press, 2004); both the video and companion text are available from www.amazon.com at the time of this printing.

Literacy videos from *Teaching for Deep Comprehension: A Reading Workshop Approach* by Linda J. Dorn and Carla Soffos (Portland, ME: Stenhouse Publishers, 2005).

This Web site has a range of videos of teaching (all levels and subject areas) and other materials of teaching practice: http://gallery.carnegiefoundation.org/insideteaching.

ABOUT THE AUTHORS

ELIZABETH A. CITY helps educators improve learning and teaching through leadership development, the strategic use of data and resources, and instructional rounds networks. She is Director of Instructional Strategy at the Executive Leadership Program for Educators at Harvard University and is a faculty member at Boston's School Leadership Institute. Liz has served as a teacher, an instructional coach, and a principal. She holds a doctorate in administration, planning, and social policy from the Harvard Graduate School of Education. Her publications include *Resourceful Leadership: Tradeoffs and Tough Decisions on the Road to School Improvement* (Harvard Education Press, 2008); *The Teacher's Guide to Leading Student-Centered Discussions: Talking About Texts in the Classroom*, coauthored with Michael S. Hale (Corwin Press, 2006); and *Data Wise: A Step-by-Step Guide to Using Assessment Results to Improve Teaching and Learning,* coedited with Kathryn Parker Boudett and Richard J. Murnane (Harvard Education Press, 2005).

RICHARD F. ELMORE is the Gregory R. Anrig Professor of Educational Leadership at Harvard University. He is also codirector of the Connecticut Superintendents' Network, a community of practice for superintendents engaged in the improvement of instruction, sponsored by the Connecticut Center for School Change. He is a member of the faculty on the Executive Leadership Program for Educators, which builds on several prior initiatives at Harvard's Graduate School of Education, Business School, and Kennedy School of Government, and works with state commissioners of education and school superintendents along with their leadership teams and key stakeholders. He holds a bachelor's degree in political science from Whitman College, Walla Walla, Washington; a master's degree in political science from the Claremont Graduate School, Claremont, California; and a doctorate in educational policy from the Harvard Graduate School of Education. His publications include *School Reform from the Inside Out: Policy, Practice, and Performance* (Harvard Education Press, 2004); *Restructuring in the Classroom*, coauthored with Penelope L. Peterson and Sarah J. McCarthey (Jossey-Bass, 1996); "Getting to Scale with Good Educational Practice," *Harvard Educational Review* (Spring, 1996); and "Investing in Teacher Learning: Staff Development and Instructional Improvement in Community School District #2, New York City" (National Commission on Teaching & America's Future and CPRE, 1997). He is coeditor, with Bruce Fuller and Gary Orfield, of *Who Chooses, Who Loses? Culture, Institutions, and the Unequal Effects of*

School Choice (Teachers College Press, 1996); and, with Susan Fuhrman, *The Governance of Curriculum* (ASCD, 1994).

SARAH E. FIARMAN is the acting principal of the Martin Luther King, Jr. School in Cambridge, Massachusetts. She enjoys helping educators build powerful learning communities through examining data, participating in instructional rounds, and using the Responsive Classroom approach to teaching. A former elementary school teacher and National Board Certified Teacher, Sarah is completing her doctoral degree in administration, planning, and social policy at the Harvard Graduate School of Education. She is a contributing author to several books about improving instruction, including *Data Wise in Action: Stories of Schools Using Data to Improve Teaching and Learning*, edited by Kathryn Parker Boudett and Jennifer Steele (Harvard Education Press, 2007); *Data Wise: A Step-by-Step Guide to Using Assessment Results to Improve Teaching and Learning*, edited by Kathryn Parker Boudett, Elizabeth A. City, and Richard J. Murnane (Harvard Education Press, 2005); and *Making Teaching Visible: Documenting Individual and Group Learning as Professional Development* (Project Zero, Harvard Graduate School of Education, 2003).

LEE TEITEL helps schools and school systems improve instruction and increase organizational capacity through leadership development, partnering, and the use of networks. In addition to teaching courses in these areas as a faculty member at the Harvard Graduate School of Education, he was founding director and currently serves as a faculty senior associate of the Executive Leadership Program for Educators. This innovative collaboration joins faculty from three of Harvard's graduate schools with commissioners, superintendents, and other school leaders in six states to bring high-quality teaching and learning to scale in urban and high-need districts. As a consultant, Lee has worked with numerous districts, individual partnerships, networks, and a statewide school- and teacher-improvement effort. He has set up learning networks for principals and superintendents in several states and, for the last four years, has cofacilitated instructional rounds networks with superintendents and other school leaders in Connecticut, Ohio, and Iowa. Sample publications include, on leadership networks, "Changing the Culture of Peer Support for Superintendents," forthcoming in *School Administrator* (2009); on leadership development, *Mapping the Terrain of 'Alternative' Leadership Education: Lessons for Universities* (Phi Delta Kappan, 2006); and on partnerships, *The Professional Development School Handbook: Starting, Sustaining, and Assessing Partnerships that Improve Student Learning* (Corwin Press, 2003).

INDEX

Information contained in figures and tables are indicated by an italic *f* and *t* respectively.